THE
Archive Photographs
SERIES

SEABURN
AND
ROKER

Welcome to

ROKER and
SEABURN

With the compliments of the Seaside Development and Entertainments Committee
Entertainments and Publicity Manager: W. N. JACKSON, F.Inst.M.E.M.

An illustration from the 1947 Guide to Roker and Seaburn. *Oh I do like to be beside the seaside …*

THE
Archive Photographs
SERIES

SEABURN
AND
ROKER

Compiled by
Pat O'Brien and Peter Gibson

TEMPUS

First published 1997
Copyright © Pat O'Brien and Peter Gibson, 1997

Tempus Publishing Limited
The Mill, Brimscombe Port, Stroud,
Gloucestershire GL5 2QG

ISBN 0 7524 1040 7

Typesetting and origination by
Tempus Publishing Limited
Printed in Great Britain by
Midway Clark Printing, Wiltshire

The miniature railway at Seaburn, 30 June 1968. The popular 'little railway' was owned by Sunderland Corporation. The cafe in the background was another council venture after the Second World War. *Photograph by Ian S. Carr.*

Contents

Acknowledgements   6

The Playground of the People   7

1.   **Roker**   9
The Pier … Holey Rock … Bede's Cross … Cat and Dog Steps … Cannonball Rocks … Cliff Park … Pierrots … Nudists …

2.   **Roker Park**   35
The Babbies … Ravine Bridges … Illuminations … Legend of Spottie … Skeleton Discovery … Football Ground … Monument Fountain … Closing Bell …

3.   **Seaburn**   45
Sea Lane … Tentland … Bent's Farm … Corporation's Ambitions … Bellerby's Amusements … Guidi's … H.M.S. Sentinel … Seaburn Camp …

4.   **Seaburn After the War**   59
Beaches Opened Again … 'Master Plan' … Sunspot of the North East … Modest Developments … Huge Crowds … Lost Children … Failure and Decline … Boxing Day Dip…

5.   **Our Entertainment**   77
Jumbo … 1950s Illuminations … Big Top … Village Queen … The Fair … Big Dipper … Sand Artists … Bonnie Prince Charlie …

6.   **Notarianni's**   95
A Move to Sunderland … The Family … Finest Ices … Knickerbocker Glory … War, Internment and Separation … Cornets and Monkey's Blood .. A Place to Meet… 1950s Crowds …

7.   **Life Savers**   103
Roker Volunteers … Heroism … Shipwrecks … Breeches Buoy … The Orion … Billy Burton … Tragedy at Roker … Lifeguards …

8.   **Family Album and Memories**   113
Donkey Rides … Candy Floss … Toffee Apples … Bathing Belles … Happy Days … Sandy Sandwiches … Hot Rice … Olive Oil and Vinegar …

Acknowledgements

The authors wish to sincerely thank the following people, organisations and sources for help during the research and production of this book. Andrew Clark, North East editor for The Chalford Publishing Company for his support and guidance. Julie Burlinson who word processed the manuscript. North East Press (*Sunderland Echo*) for allowing us to publish their photographs. Tyne and Wear Museums Service (Sunderland Museum and Art Gallery). Neil Sinclair, museum staff, and the museum attendants for their help and consideration. Sunderland City Library (Local Studies), Phil Hall, Ashley Sutherland and the rest of the staff in a busy Local Studies room. Martin Routledge, Marie O'Reilly, Mark Gibson, Irene Gibson and Alan Brett for their comments on the text. Lynda Davison's collection, May Cook and the late Dick Cook, Meg Robertson, Pauline Tait, Joe Salkeld's collection, Alan Tedder, Mickey Taggart, Frank Phillips jnr, Nicola Lamb, Billy Bellerby and the Bellerby fairground family, Judith Balzi, Kath Fenwick, Ann Ray, Cara Kingsley, Gino Notarianni, Egideo Notarianni and the Notarianni family, Fred Roberts, Norman Clark, Tommy Cavanagh and Roker Volunteer Life Brigade, Alan Gelder, Joan Bainbridge, Charles R. Riddell, Dorothie E. Stalton, Margaret Lennon, Mrs Ethel Wilson, Stanley Heavisides, Mrs Esther Gibson, Barbara Johnson, Betty Watson, Margaret Thynne, Jean and Stan Fowler, Barbara Collar, Roy Elwen, the staff of Hendon Branch Library, Doreen Talbot from *The Echo*, Terry Gibson, Donna Gibson, Christine Nixon, Juanita Sloma, Simon Jeffrey, Ann and Jim Hughes, Evelyn Arkle, Lorna Storey. Several official guides to Sunderland, several official guides to Roker and Seaburn, Annual Reports of Sunderland Volunteer Life Brigade, *Sunderland Echo*, *Sunderland Herald*, *Sunderland Times*, several Sunderland Year Books. Finally we wish to thank our partners, Irene and Gordon for tolerating the workload and 'the mess'.

Holey Roker, *c.* 1930. (See also pp. 15-18.)

The Playground of the People

Every Wearsider has memories of 'the beach'. A stroll along Sunderland's seafront not only reveals a pleasant combination of natural and man-made features, but it can provoke memories of a busy seaside resort which buzzed with activity on a hot summer's day. Packed buses unloaded excited children at the terminus next to Hastings' post office. There was the distinct smell of sea air and sea weed; fishing with hand-lines from the pier; or willicking on Whitburn Steel. There are memories of a week long stay with the school at Seaburn Camp, as well as the fair, boating pool, miniature railway, or simply playing or relaxing on the beach.

Roker and Seaburn have a relatively short history. One of the earliest references is the well documented fact that the Abbs family was granted land at Roker in 1587 on condition they provided six soldiers to help defend the river mouth from attack. Abbs Battery can be seen perched on Holey Rock on several photographs in this book. Despite a military presence, Roker remained a quiet rural area popular with smugglers. In the 1840s Roker Terrace was built which included the Roker Hotel and Monkwearmouth Baths. However, it was not until the latter part of the nineteenth century that the gradual increase in the importance of leisure gained momentum. Roker Park opened in 1880, a road bridge was constructed over the ravine, and postcards from the turn of the century provide us with visual evidence of the popularity of Roker.

The history of Seaburn as a resort is much shorter than that of Roker's. Most of Seaburn was in the Parish of Fulwell and under the control of Sunderland Rural District. Again, postcards provide evidence of the growing popularity of Seaburn in the 1920s, especially with day visitors arriving on charabanc trips. The approaches to Seaburn were favourable compared to the steep approaches to Roker beach. However, the Rural District Council did not have the resources to develop the seafront and when Sunderland Corporation absorbed Fulwell in 1928 there were ambitions to make Sunderland into the biggest seaside resort town on the North East Coast. Nonetheless, *The Echo* became impatient at the slow progress and commented in May 1930: 'Sunderland has on its doorstep a potential goldmine as a seaside resort. When will it be recognised?' Over-ambitious plans produced in 1930 were stifled by protests from the Rate-payers' Association and moderates in the council chamber. Furthermore, a new housing estate was emerging at Seaburn (see the photograph on p. 52) and the residents would have to be considered when developing the resort. Lane Fox and Company, the Norton-on-Tees builders, advertised new houses for sale in 1939 on Seaburn Estate and Dykelands Road for £595, £475 and £410.

Sensible expansion blueprints evolved for the seafront and in the 1930s new promenades were built; new approach roads were constructed; a new shopping complex went up in Queen's Parade; a permanent site was found for the fairground; Seaburn Hotel and Seaburn Hall were built; and the popularity of the twin resorts was boosted in 1938 when workers' experienced their first ever week's holiday with pay.

The Second World War put an end to further work and after the war the Seaside Development Committee of Sunderland Corporation announced some incredible schemes to turn Seaburn and Roker into one of the top four British seaside resorts. However, the ambitious schemes did not materialise and they were replaced with realistic improvements in the 1950s. In 1953 workers were awarded two weeks summer holiday with pay and Seaburn and Roker were the places to go for Wearsiders during 'shipyard fortnight'.

Seaburn declined in the late 1970s and much of the land between Seaburn Camp and Dykelands Road deteriorated into an eyesore. Nevertheless, the late 1980s saw a recovery and the crowds returned: the illuminations were restored in 1986; the derelict area was rejuvenated; Morrisons Supermarket was built; the fairground was moved to the front; the Pullman Lodge Hotel was constructed and Seaburn Centre opened in 1990. The late 1980s also saw Seaburn Hotel substantially improved and renamed; and moreover, dare we include the erection of the fountain as an improvement?

This book has been divided into sections for the convenience of readers. Many of the rare photographs, however, can comfortably fit into more than one section. The content briefly examines the development of Seaburn and Roker. We also look at our entertainment, the well remembered Notarianni family business, and the heroism of life savers. The final section - 'Family Album and Memories' allows us to share the personal reminiscences of Wearsiders and ex-pats. A common theme emerges from these memories of a strong sense of community spirit that existed in the suburbs of Sunderland and which was displayed on the beaches. Families, extended families, friends and neighbours assembled in groups at their favourite spot to enjoy the simple pleasures of a day at the seaside.

In 1923 a local businessman aptly referred to Sunderland's seafront as 'the playground of the people'. An appropriate epithet for the decades that followed. In recent years, of course, people have found other ways to spend their leisure time, and apart from the successful annual air show, the summer now passes rather quietly at Seaburn and Roker. Some of our well-meaning forefathers had great plans for the twin resorts, but did we really want a Blackpool, a Whitley Bay or a Scarborough on our doorstep? Perhaps because the seafront is there for us every day is the reason why we take too much for granted to appreciate what we have here. In spite of 1997 criticism that sea water off the coast of Roker is 'still not clean enough' our seaside is the envy of inner city folk. Sunderland's seafront is a clean and healthy open area where we can find 'our space'.

Lessons can be learnt from history and a policy of modest improvement should be preferred over ambitious schemes of the like which caused problems in the 1970s. It is essential that Seaburn and Roker continue to be cared for, nurtured and preserved for Wearsiders as THE PLAYGROUND OF THE PEOPLE.

Pauline Clow (now Tait), aged nine, and her cousin David Copeland, aged six, on Seaburn beach in 1949. Pauline lived in Essex and each year visited relatives in Fulwell. Pauline recalls: 'Spending a holiday on the beach at Seaburn was a real treat because we lived inland in a small village. I can remember the donkeys and their distinct smell. The ride was uncomfortable but exciting with my slippery wet cossy, and my bare feet in the stirrups, I always felt that I was going to fall off.'

One
Roker

The Pier ... Holey Rock ... Bede's Cross ... Cat and Dog Steps ... Cannonball Rocks ... Cliff Park ... Pierrots ... Nudists ...

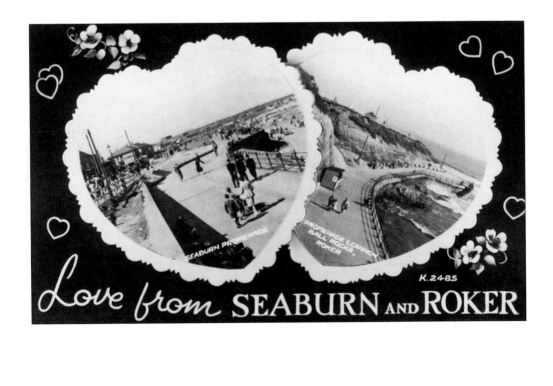

The construction of the lower promenade at Roker on 6 May 1886. On the far left is the Holey Rock. Roker Pier is being built on the far right. The large crane was a landmark on the pier for two decades. Workmen can be seen busy at work in the foreground on the promenade's foundations. By May, when this photograph was taken, it was warm work and discarded black coats are dotted around the sand. But earlier in the year working conditions were very much different when it was reported: 'They worked on the banks till they could scarcely walk home from the cold.' These were men from the ranks of the unemployed who walked miles from all parts of Sunderland in the hope of a day's work. The Roker Improvement Works had began in January 1886 during a recession in trade, as an alternative to stone breaking and the workhouse. The local government board in London had sanctioned the borrowing of £7,000 by the Corporation of Sunderland to carry out the work. The rate of pay was 2s 6d (12½pence) per day or 15 shillings (75p) per week. There was a six day working week and about 200 men were employed on the scheme. Men were glad of the work to avoid the humiliation of tickets to the workhouse for themselves and their families, which would mean becoming pauperised and losing the right to vote. However, severe weather at Roker caused stoppages and the men were sent home regularly with no pay. In March 1886 disgruntled men employed on the promenade scheme attended a mass meeting in West Park. An elected chairman addressed the men as 'fellow paupers' who couldn't get work anywhere. There was general approval of the chairman's comment that they all should have applied to the Guardians to enter the workhouse with their wives and children instead of seeking work at Roker where the actual working days had been so few. One man with five children had received one day's work in a fortnight, and another had earned 2s 6d in three weeks. There was no other source of income and the chairman stated that families were now practically starving. The bitterness at the meeting in March 1886 overflowed as men aired their grievances: money put aside for the promenade development was being spent on foremen's wages who were given work while the rest of the men were sent home. And furthermore, that there were those 'at Roker who did not want them there because they were not their kith and kin'. Alderman Bell assured the men in a report read by the chairman that matters would improve and there would be more days of work available for the men.

New Pier, Roker

RELIABLE SERIES 715

The opening of Roker Pier on 23 September 1903. Lord Durham laid the last stone on that day and the ceremony was witnessed by a large crowd of VIPs and Wearside businessmen. Several thousand spectators lined the terrace above Roker beach and the beautiful weather complemented colourful flags, banners and music from the band of the Northumberland Hussars. Lord Durham in his speech described the pier as '... a magnificent ornament to Sunderland.'

Work begins on Roker Pier in 1885. The site had a foundation of rock but before building could begin, sand up to sixteen feet deep was removed. Sand beneath the waterline was sucked up by the vessel *Sandrail*. The barge *Concrete* then laid 56 ton and 116 ton bags of dry powdered concrete cement on the rocks which dried solid beneath the waves. The top surface of the concrete foundation was levelled just above the low water mark, and the huge granite faced blocks were lowered into place by a 45 ton radial crane. This large crane can be seen on the pier on p.11.

Postcard, postmarked 9 October 1942. To Mrs S. N. Jones, 23 Church Street, Exmouth, Devon. 'Dearest Kath, Spending the day here but the weather is not too hot. In fact I have had to wear my great coat. Writing this while we are awaiting dinner. I am with a chap from our hut. We shall probably go to the pictures this afternoon. Has Edward got his bike yet? Well fairly cheerio. Love, Stanley xxx'. When Roker Pier was completed in September 1903, at a cost of £290,000, it was acclaimed an engineering wonder. The gigantic arm breakwater had taken eighteen years to build, and the work was designed and supervised from beginning to end by River Wear Commissioners' engineer Henry Hay Wake.

Postcard, postmarked 14 June 1916. To Mrs H. J. Braithwaite. 'Dear Braithwaite, I hope you have better weather than we have had here since Saturday, very rough winds and cold, with rough seas washing over the pier, and foam over the top of the lighthouse. Sea grand to look at but awful to be on with a small boat. Trade going on as usual. I have been here a week, shall stay till next week. Kind regards to all. I am yours truly. J Smith'.

Lighthouse. Roker.

The lighthouse, *c*. 1910. In 1915 heavy seas damaged the pier and the sea flooded the tunnel trapping a navel signalman and four soldiers in the lighthouse for one day. The storm receded and the soldiers were able to walk along the pier to obtain provisions. In another unfortunate incident during the First World War a soldier was washed off the pier and lost during heavy seas. In 1931 the lighthouse signal was changed from gas to electricity, and what was described as an 'ingenious mechanism' was fitted as a precaution against failure. The gas supply was kept in reserve and in the event of failure of the electricity the burner would be automatically lit. An alarm panel was set up in the bedroom of the lighthouse keeper to warn him of any problems in the lighthouse.

Lighthouse keeper William Emmerson, aged fifty-eight, with the recently installed wireless set in March 1948. The up-to-date wireless equipment allowed the transmission of correct bearings to ships passing by the lighthouse. Mr Emmerson could also receive messages. If the lighthouse lamp failed, and the alarm went off in Mr Emmerson's home at the shore end of the pier, he could normally make it to the lighthouse in ten minutes. In March 1948 William Emmerson had been lighthouse keeper for twenty-seven years and he recalled his worst experience which occurred in 1937: 'A very stormy night eleven years ago I was kept awake all night in my home expecting every minute to hear the alarm bell ring. Mountainous waves smashed the subway skylights and water poured into the tunnel. It was impossible to reach the lighthouse along the top of the pier, so I was compelled to don a divers suit and wade through the flooded subway - a three hour journey'.

14

Holey Rock in the 1920s, looking west. Holey Rock is remembered with affection with the cliff face resembling an elephant. It was a landmark and an integral part of Roker where the action of the sea had created a natural beauty. Sometimes holiday makers, assuming its name derived from some supernatural source, chipped small parts of it away to take home as souvenirs. The name Holey Rock, of course, derives from the numerous caves and passageways which honeycombed this section of Roker cliffs. In April 1930 Sunderland Parks Committee proposed to block up the entrances to Holey Rock with concrete at a cost of £1,000, but the request was turned down by the council. By February 1934, however, there were serious fears about safety and members of the Seaside Development Committee inspected the rock and found that parts of it were unsafe. There was a reluctance once again to spend so much money on concrete to block up the caves. Shortly afterwards a combination of storms and spring tides caused falls of rocks inside the caves and also undermined the cliffs in the vicinity of Holey Rock. A decision was made on 5 April 1934 to close the caves permanently and to immediately scale away dangerous portions of the cliff.

Holey Rock Roker, resembling Elephant. M. 36

A postcard showing Holey Rock and postmarked 17 November 1904. At the extreme left a pierrot group, 'The Jumbles', entertain the crowd. (See p. 19.)

An unusual view of the interior of Holey Rock - an adventure playground for youngsters. When closure was ordered the caves were blocked up by iron railings. In April 1934 the Seaside Development Committee announced a scheme to set the unemployed to work joining up the promenade and sea wall on either side of Holey Rock. Two options were considered; to cut through Holey Rock, or to demolish it. The latter was decided upon after taking into consideration recent fears about its stability.

Arthur Jeffrey (1864-1936), on the right, the Sunderland Council Alderman, bathing at Holey Rock with his family, the Panton's from Deptford, in August 1932. Arthur Jeffrey also ran the entertainments and tea room at Holey Rock during the summer months, as well as a shop in the town centre. For a period of time he ran the Avenue Theatre which is now Vaux's Avenue Theatre Bottling House.

Pick and shovel work on the south side of Holey Rock in June 1936. Material is being removed in preparation to build the retaining wall. A disturbing discovery was made during the demolition of Holey Rock. An unexploded bomb dropped by a Zeppelin in the First World War was unearthed. 'Block Yard' wrote to *The Echo* in February 1973 of memories of Roker in the 1920s and '30s: '… Holey Rock, a major attraction, going in and out of the arches, then on to the front, staring with wonder at the elastic-skin man, who pulled his chest skin over his face, or the man who swallowed three feet of chain while the bathers were going in and out of the bathing cabins nearby …'

Demolition of the Holey Rock begins in June 1936. This is the last view of 'an old friend' to many Wearsiders. In the background is the retaining wall which would be extended in connection with the Holey Rock scheme. The new wall made safe the cliffs to the north of Holey Rock where there had been falls of limestone.

Holey Rock corner in the 1920s. On the left is the Holey Rock Dance and Tea Gardens which opened on 15 May 1922 on the site of the Jumbles Pierrot Troupe. Thousands of people attended the opening ceremony, and many couples danced throughout the opening evening to the local band 'Cameo'. Abbs Battery can be seen on Holey Rock.

The scene taken from the same position as above in the late 1930s.

The 'now' scene of Holey Rock corner in March 1997.

The Jumbles Pierrot Troupe, *c*. 1904. Pierrot troupes were popular performers at seaside resorts and Jumbles Concert Party was a feature near the Holey Rock before the First World War. The first troupe, led by Leonard Thiel, performed from a covered stage. Spectators sat on seats enclosed by a low wooden fence, but many people watched the show from outside the perimeter fence free of charge (see p. 15). In May 1977 eighty-three-year-old James D. Todd recalled: 'Lionel Braham, a member of the troupe, was tall with a powerful baritone. When the wind was in a certain direction he would be heard quite distinctly if you stood on the park bridge near Ravine Terrace. I took parcels of print to Holey Rock for the troupe's programmes when I was thirteen-years-old and Mr Thiel and Mr Braham would ask if I wanted to stay to watch the show. I never refused. One of the troupe in pierrot costume would collect coppers from spectators in his inverted cone hat.' The troupe later became known as 'Biddlecombe's Jumbles'.

An interesting and popular postcard, postmarked 2 April 1912 and worth repeating here. Notice that everyone is wearing a hat, and the barefoot newspaper boy on the right. To: Mr J Wilkinson, Helmington House, Hunwich Lane, Willington, Durham: 'Arrived here about 10 a.m. on Sat. Weather not good but not very bad. Went to the Empire on Sat night and to the Palace last night. I quite enjoyed myself. It's all right going out like that at night, but it is very slow here during the day, especially when it is raining. What have you been doing with yourself. I expect to return home tomorrow afternoon and hope to see you. I will come across.'

Roker sands, c. 1910. Holey Rock is in the background, and beyond Holey Rock are the Cannonball Rocks before the promenade was built.

Roker sands and pier about 1910. The pier formed a popular promenade up until 1939. Maintenance had practically ceased during the war years. The sea had done so much damage that there wasn't the funds available to carry out necessary repair work to make the pier safe for the public, consequently, it remained closed after the war.

The sands and Holey Rock in the 1920s. The wooden huts on the promenade advertises tea at two pence per cup and hot water. Further on, ices are for sale, and the next hut bears the name 'Notarianni' on the roof. Next to Notarianni's are some small children's rides. A better view of the rides can be seen on p. 22.

The beach photographer at work at Roker, *c.* 1930. This is possibly the same man who is caught on the postcard photographer's shot of Holey Rock on p. 6. In May 1930 the Roker Protection and Improvement Society was formed at a meeting in Holey Rock Pavilion. There was concern that Roker sands, which belonged to the people and was a priceless natural asset, was being destroyed. The River Wear Commissioners were responsible for the beach and were selling the sand to builders. Arthur Jeffrey chaired the meeting and stated the object of the organisation 'was to protest against the despoiling of Roker'. It was pointed out that so much sand had been taken away in carts many areas of Roker beach had been turned to stones.

A scene from the 1920s. The Beach Cafe is at the bottom of the path. The advertisement reads: 'Grills served all day on the Verandah. High Class Cafe.' (Also see p. 28.)

Whitburn Bay in 1886 by William Crosby (1830-1910). This fascinating painting shows Roker in the foreground, and Seaburn beyond as a quiet rural area with a scattering of farmhouses. Whitburn Village is in the distance.

An interesting comparison with the upper illustration, *c*. 1960. The area has become a popular sun trap at Roker as part of the well established twin resorts.

The Cannonball Rocks at Roker, c. 1900, before the promenade was built. This area became known as the Cat and Dog Steps. In December 1922 concern was raised to the threatened destruction of the unique Cannonball Rocks by covering them with a promenade - work that had been created for the unemployed. Although much of the rock in the photograph was removed or covered by the much needed promenade, the huge lump on the right protrudes today from the sea wall.

Roker by the Sea Sunderland.
Snapshotted one lovely
autumn morning up
September 1903 L. W.

A close-up of the bottom of the steps shown in the above photograph. Notice the drainage hole in the wall. Water from the cliff top seems to have found its way to the sea here and provided a natural channel in the cliffs. 'Lettie' sent this postcard to her sister: '... This is one of my very own postcards, how do you like it? It is one of my last summer plates. Hold the card facing you and the figure on your left is Cissy Laidler of Berwick. The figure on your right is my friend Miss Louie Taylor (Emily Taylor's sister). We are all well and trust that you are the same. With love from all ...' Some of the message appears on the front of the 'one off' postcard.

An artists impression of Parson's Boathouse at Roker which was built in 1876. The wooden structure was actually a small tea room owned by William Hobson and probably derived its name from the cannonball rocks, known as Parson's Rocks, upon which the rear of the building rested. There was also a boathouse nearby. The front of the building faced the sea and was supported by wooden piles sunk into the sand. Parson's Boathouse was an oddity which attracted day visitors to the quietness of rural Roker. The tea room was entered from the beach by wooden steps which were covered by the sea at high tide. Waves sometimes smashed into the front door and it seems remarkable that the building stood for twenty-eight years. There was also a rear door which led to the cliff top. In 1904 the little tea room was demolished to make way for a promenade.

Roker beach, *c.* 1948.

Time to relax, and to read, and to knit, and to chat, and to eat, and to enjoy the sun on the Cat and Dog Steps promenade in 1971.

'Little tinkers' skinny dippin' in the sea at Roker earlier this century. In April 1979 the Central Council for British Naturalism made a request to Sunderland Council for permission to open a nudist colony on a section of Seaburn beach. The request was turned down and the council stated categorically that no nude bathing would be permitted on Sunderland beaches.

Mr Payne, aged seventy-five, and his wife, outside of their caravan home not far from the sea at Roker in 1931. Although retired they had lived at Roker for ten years where Mr Payne had been the owner of a roundabout on the lower promenade. He was born in Hull but was orphaned when he was very young. 'I was only nine (in 1865) when I went to sea on a fishing smack,' said Mr Payne in May 1931. 'Sometimes the voyages lasted as long as twelve weeks - twelve weeks of agony for us youngsters. We were poorly fed and hard worked. I can remember the salt water and the cold winds splitting my hands so badly that I could put a threepenny piece in the cracks. When I was about seventeen I heard that there was money to be made in the fair business, so I spent the little money that I had managed to save in the purchase of three small swings, which I took to fairs in various parts of the country.' The Paynes became well known among fair families and Mr Payne thought that caravan life on the road was a healthy way of life.

The paddling pool in the late 1940s. Notice the miniature railway on the promenade.

Three thresher sharks, caught by the four man crew of the *Thankful* off the coast of Roker, created an interest on Roker beach in August 1929. The *Thankful*, skippered by Phil Smith, had caught five sharks that year. The biggest, caught in July, was eighteen feet long and weighed one ton, but that might have been the one that got away! Another shark caught in November was a youngster, nine feet long and was hauled on board by a block and tackle. Phil Smith said: 'We knew that there was a shark following us because we landed three codfish which had been bitten in half … The shark had eaten a codfish which we had caught, and then was caught on the same hook.' There have been other visitors to Roker and Seaburn over the years. In the nineteenth century porpoises are recorded as frequent visitors, but in March 1976 when three porpoises were washed up at Seaburn their sudden appearance was considered a rarity and a mystery. In July 1977 people were advised to keep out of the sea after local fishermen had caught giant jellyfish in their nets. Some of them were three feet in diameter with fourteen feet tentacles.

Lockhart's Cafe, *c.* 1910. The 1938 Guide to Roker and Seaburn advertises the building as the Beach Cafe on the lower promenade, Roker: 'Parties catered for. Seating accommodation 400. All foods kept in refrigerators. Popular prices …' T. Crawford was the proprietor. The building later housed night clubs: The Rokoko was opened in 1964 and in the 1970s it was known as The Beach Club. There was another name change to Rumours night club and in August 1987 it was gutted by fire causing damage estimated at £100,000. The building was demolished. A pub was built on the site which opened as Nelson's. The pub is now called The Smugglers.

Roker, c. 1970. Seaburn was the focus of attention for new developments after the Second World War and Roker suffered a decline in popularity. The steep approaches and the untidy Blockyard eyesore were two of several other reasons blamed for turning Wearsiders and day visitors to Seaburn for their pleasure. Other reasons included: Holey Rock had been demolished, there were no more daily concerts at Roker Park bandstand, the pierrots and other amusements had disappeared, and the pier had been closed to the public. Furthermore, Roker Gill sewer construction in 1950 and ugly sewer pipes added to the unattractive look. 'Who would bring a child here?' asked a Roker tradesman.

Members of Green Street Hebron Envangelistical church caused a spectacle at Roker between the piers in May 1934 when they held a baptism service in the sea. The unusual scene attracted five hundred spectators to the beach and Pastor Entwistle spoke from a raft in the water: 'Our motive for holding this service of baptism by immersion is found in the New Testament. We have found that the early Christian Church baptized by immersion. We can find no evidence of sprinkling.' The Revd Entwistle and his assistant Mr J. Sinclair wore special black rubber vestments to baptise several people.

THE PROMENADE AND HOLEY ROCK

A postcard from around 1920. The residents of seafront houses at Roker had a lucky escape on 17 November 1952 when a Meteor jet exploded in mid-air. A spluttering noise was heard and the jet was seen to turn towards the sea as if to avoid hitting the houses. Seconds later the Meteor disintegrated showering Seaburn and Roker with debris and narrowly missing several people on the ground. The pilot was never found.

Roker Hotel, c. 1910. Construction of the hotel and attached Monkwearmouth Baths began in 1840. However, a curious incident occurred in November 1840 when the front of the baths was blown down. Fortunately, none of the workmen were injured as all but two of them were watching the wreck of the *Syria*. The baths and hotel were completed and offered for lease in February 1842. Sea water was obtained for the baths by the use of a powerful pump. In April 1842 Edward Brown became the first tenant.

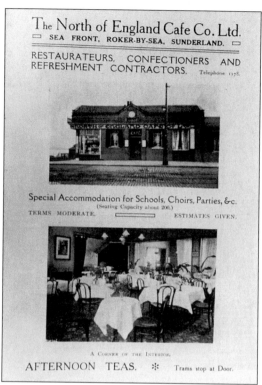

An advertisement for the North of England Cafe, c. 1914. The cafe stood on the corner opposite the Roker Voluntary Life Brigade Watchhouse. There was seating accommodation for two hundred and the company catered specially for schools, choirs and parties. Trams conveniently stopped at the door and the cafe was particularly proud of their 'dainty afternoon teas'. In April 1935 the building was sold to the Sunderland Christian Science Society. They converted one of the large rooms to a church. Notice the South Pier in the background on the left of the top photograph.

The Bungalow Cafe, c. 1910. This popular little cafe, which overlooks the harbour and Roker Pier, is a well remembered landmark and it is an integral part of Sunderland's seafront. Alan Gelder has been in business there since 1962. Alan recalls: 'When I first came here business in the cafe was so hectic that we would sell £25 worth of hot water in a day. We charged sixpence per pot.' Around 1988 Tyne and Wear Development Corporation made a compulsory purchase order and they had plans to demolish the building. Local people organised a campaign to save the cafe and 5,000 people signed a petition. The Gelders received letters of support from as far away as Canada and Australia. In 1997 Alan Gelder bought the Bungalow Cafe.

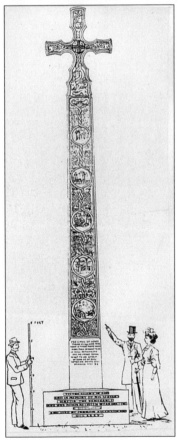

The Bede memorial, a beautifully sculptured cross dedicated to Sunderland's most famous son. It was unveiled by the Archbishop of York, Dr Maclagen on 11 October 1904 in front of a large crowd of about 5,000 people. The cross was removed to a place of safety at the outbreak of the First Word War. It was then replaced to its prominent position on Cliff Park after hostilities ceased, to once again become 'a beacon stone, a standard to be far seen by those who sail the sea, plough the land or who are on their all-too-short holiday …' Evacuation of the cross occurred again at the beginning of another world war when it was dismantled and placed in Eden Vale corporation yard. In 1949 discussions took place about re-erecting the Bede cross. The parks committee intended it to be part of a proposed garden of remembrance in St Peter's churchyard, but the seaside development committee decided the original site overlooking the North Sea would be the most effective setting.

An illustration of the Bede Memorial Cross from the 1905 Sunderland Year Book. The cross is shown in proportion to a man holding a six feet measuring pole. The inscription was carved in the base block: 'To the glory of God and in memory of His servant Bede, 673-735.' The architect was Clement Hodges.

The town council approved the re-erection of the cross to its former site and work is taking place in April 1949. The memorial consists of three sections - the base, which had been left on the site during the war and was damaged, and two parts for the cross. The cross too, was in a bad state of repair after lying in the builders yard. Restoration work took place by the council after it was in place.

Cliff Park, Roker, looking north in about 1910. A section of the promenade on the right is being constructed, and building materials are stored on Cliff Park. Beyond the stone blocks a horse and cart are laden with bags of cement. An unusual event occurred at 7 p.m. on 31 July 1946. 'Sunderland Sands Mission' opened with a procession of five hundred people from St Andrew's church to Cliff Park. The impressive spectacle was headed by the Sunderland Transport Band. The Bishop of Durham's first mission at Sunderland was part of a national aim of the Church of England for the conversion of the country, and to take the church to the people at seaside resorts. Holiday makers, local people and visitors to the seafront made up a crowd of about 1,500 people who heard the Bishop of Durham speak from a form in front of a large marquee. The week long services became popular and at the opening of the third sands mission in July 1948, eight hundred church goers from twenty-three local churches took part in the procession from St Andrew's church to Cliff Park. The open air service was heard by about two thousand people.

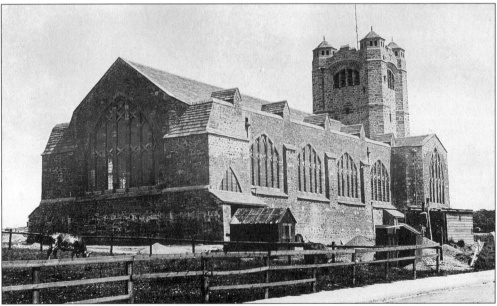

St Andrew's church, around 1910, was the base for the sands missions at Sunderland after the war.

Two
Roker Park

The Babbies ... Ravine Bridges ... Illuminations ...
Legend of Spottie ... Skeleton Discovery ... Football
Ground ... Monument Fountain ... Closing Bell ...

I'M GETTING
ROUND AT ROKER

This is the " stile " to spoon, you see,
So happy together, both he and she ;
While underneath, if you will pry,
Will be found the beauties that round them lie.

An undated view earlier this century of the beach side entrance to Roker Park, showing the two bridges over the ravine. Notice, the underground 'gentlemen's lavatories' on the left. A 'ladies' sign is attached to the cliff at the other end. The pedestrian Ravine Bridge was built around 1901 and is a notable characteristic of Roker Park. It was almost demolished, however, after it became unsafe and was closed to the public. A public campaign in 1981 saved the bridge, repairs were carried out and it was opened again. Roker Park ravine is a place of natural beauty and interest and provided an ideal setting for the Corporation to lay out a park in 1880. Sir Hedworth Williamson donated the land but he made an agreement with Sunderland that they must build a bridge across the ravine to make a continuous road along the seafront. That bridge is shown above. Roker ravine was also known as 'smugglers haunt' and there are legends of underground tunnels stretching from the caves to Hylton Castle, Monkwearmouth and Southwick. High import duties of the 1600s and 1700s encouraged widespread smuggling of alcohol and linen. Fishermen, keelmen and bargemen avoided customs officers to bring illegal goods ashore to a sympathetic public. The isolation and quietness of Roker was an ideal place to land and hide contraband in the numerous caves. Smuggling was common knowledge to all classes of Wearsiders but many turned 'a blind eye'. One of the numerous caves in Roker ravine was the home of Spottie who was said to have been an eighteenth century sailor whose ship was wrecked off the coast of Sunderland. Tales of Spottie are varied but it is generally thought that he was French or Spanish and communicated with locals by using signs because he couldn't speak English. He survived by begging food or by doing odd jobs for local farmers and he was given the name 'Spottie' because of the spotted shirt he always wore. The legend of Spottie tells of ships he lured onto the rocks by lighting a fire to fool sailors into believing they were heading towards harbour lights. He then looted the cargo of the wrecked vessels. Spottie's strange language and appearance, as well as his reclusive way of life, caused fear of a 'bogeyman'. The women of Whitburn were said to have been so afraid of him they travelled to market in Sunderland by boat instead of walking past Spottie's Hole at Roker. However, some records reveal that Spottie was an inoffensive, reserved man whose sudden and mysterious disappearance caused speculation and so fuelled the legend.

Roker Park closing bell in the early 1960s. The inscription on the bell reads: 'Presented to the Corporation of Sunderland for Roker Park by Mr Councillor Shadforth Vice-Chairman of the Parks Committee July 1881.' The closing bell was positioned in the Dell between the two bowling greens but it was stolen in the mid to late 1960s. Roker Park Gates, which were positioned at the Roker Park Road entrance, were another feature which disappeared from the park. They were removed in October 1942 as part of the wartime scrap metal drive. The gates were a relic of old Sunderland. Before their erection at Roker they were originally the toll gates on Wearmouth Bridge.

Roker Park from the Ravine Bridge, c. 1910. Postcard to: Mrs Kettlewell, 14 Filey Terrace, Bootham, York. 'May arrived safely. Will you please send along the old bathing costume and May's bathing cap also a piece of loofah. It is glorious weather. We were by the sea this morning. We are going to this park this afternoon. I am going to write to the boys this afternoon. I have bought a deck chair which will do for Harold when we come home. Love to everybody, Phyllis.'

Roker Park bandstand, *c.* 1910. The Sunderland Year Book in 1905 recorded: 'It may be a fact that Roker has not progressed as some wished, and that it does not yet occupy a place in the forefront of English watering places, but it cannot be denied that recently its fame has much increased … Of the many changes that have been effected, none have been more appreciated than the erection of the handsome new bandstand. It is something more than ornamental for it has proved a real utility. The season of 1905 will see it illuminated by electricity.' (See also the photographs on pp. 81 and 120.)

Roker Park ravine, *c.* 1905. Perched in a commanding position on top of the rocks on the right is a life size lead figure of a woman holding a garden rake. Another life size lead figure of a countryman sharpening a scythe at the top of the other side of the ravine faced the country maiden. The countryman can be faintly seen at the extreme left edge of the photograph.

The lead statues shown in the previous photograph were known as 'the Babbies'. The country maiden is pictured above and the countryman is in the photograph below. They were presented to the people of Sunderland for display in Roker Park by the Abbs family around 1880. The Babbies had been imported from Germany and before the gift to the town they stood on either side of the gate of Monkwearmouth House in Roker Avenue - the Abbs' family home.

In September 1940 the Babbies were removed to be melted down for lead as part of the war effort. However, it was discovered that the statues were not solid lead as first thought, but were filled with packing. The actual lead content was disappointing and there was concern that the attractive and popular feature of Roker Park had been removed unnecessarily. *The Sunderland Echo* reported of the 'unhappy end of the Babbies' and: 'The passing of the Babbies will cause considerable regret among many townspeople to whom they have quite a sentimental association … Have plaster casts been taken of the statues so that they could be restored at the conclusion of war?' enquired *The Echo*.

Monument in Park, Roker. (1039.

Roker Park monument fountain, c. 1910. The drinking fountain was presented for public use in June 1881. It stands fourteen feet high and was designed and constructed by the sculptor William Borrowdale of Sunderland. In its original state water flowed constantly from four bronze lion heads and drinking cups were attached. There were four basins and four corner columns made of polished granite.

Roker Park bowling green, 1967. Roker Park Bowling Club was formed in 1883. The club celebrated its centenary in June 1983 by organising a match with the English Bowling Association. It was the first time the association had played on a Sunderland green. In the background is the keeper's lodge. The foundation stone was laid in July 1881, and a public shelter and lavatories were attached, at a total cost, including the lodge, of £550.

The boating lake, c. 1920s. During the construction of Roker Park, water which drained from Fulwell hills was redirected to supply the boating lake. There was an overflow at the bridge (shown in the photograph) which supplied the park's water fall. Notice the large stones which border the lake. These were replaced by brickwork in the 1930s. (See lower photograph on p. 43.)

Roker illuminations, late 1930s. Roker Park was first illuminated in 1936, after plans for the previous year had been cancelled owing to work on the Roker Gill sewer. 'Illuminations Fortnight' took place from 12-26 September 1936 and over 30,000 people paid to enter Roker Park during the opening weekend. Thousands waited their turn to see the characters of fairyland, and although the crowds were good humoured, policemen had to link arms to hold them back at the entrance. The 1936 illuminations were such a success that they were extended to one month in 1937.

Alice in Wonderland was an attractive feature in Roker Park illuminations in the late 1930s.

The 1938 Roker Park illuminations ran from 10 September to 9 October. Talking set pieces had been successfully introduced in 1937 and those were extended in 1938 to make the pirate cave and its sound effects the highlight of the illuminations. Other artistic attractions included the merry dell, gypsy encampment, fairy grove, Alice in Wonderland, jungle school, and oriental walk. Notarianni's sold ice cream from a kiosk and light refreshments were provided by Atkinson's of Queen's Parade, Seaburn. The Mayor, George Ford, wrote in August 1938 that the illuminations committee, chaired by Alderman T. Summerbell JP had engaged 'the very best dance bands available'. On the opening night Sunderland Constabulary Band entertained on the bandstand. From 11-17 September there was Oscar Rabin and his Romany Band; 18-24 September, Billy Gerhardi and his Orchestra; and from 2-9 October, Billy Merrin and his Commanders starred. Admission to the band enclosure was sixpence, and there was dancing nightly near the Roker Baths Road entrance to the Frisco Syncopators. Entry was one shilling.

SUNDERLAND CORPORATION

ROKER
ILLUMINATIONS
1938

SOUVENIR PROGRAMME 3D.

The castle on Roker Park pond during the illuminations, c. 1950 . The boy is Robert Logan grandson of Frank Phillips the sand artist (see p. 90, 91). A curious incident occurred in Roker Park in October 1952 when two schoolboys were digging in sand on a ledge sixteen feet up the bank side in the ravine. The boys unearthed part of a skeleton which consisted of skull, vertebrae and femur. Police investigated the find and sent the human remains to Wakefield forensic laboratory where it was determined the skeleton was at least two hundred years old. The person had been middle aged and five feet tall but the sex was not known. There were no signs of injury to the bones. Perhaps it was the remains of Spottie?

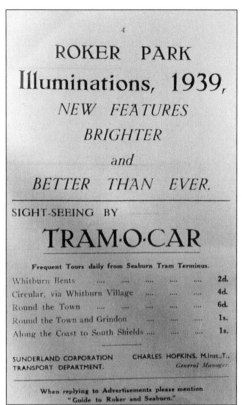

The 1939 illuminations go down as 'the lights that never were'. Although they were set up and ready for the official switch on, war was declared and the public didn't get a chance to see them. In the late 1930s the Roker illuminations were said to have been the best in Britain and even better than Blackpool's. The town had worked hard for the 1939 illuminations. Roker ravine was packed with illuminated figures and the lights stretched along 'the golden mile' to Seaburn recreation park. On 1 September the illuminations were switched on as a preview for illuminations committee members. A *Sunderland Echo* reporter was invited and described some of the scenes: '… Robbers Den in Roker ravine and see the merry men of Robin Hood's day aglow in the magic colours of fluorescent light. One moment the scene is lit with ordinary light and the next the cave is in darkness and ultra violet rays are focused on the gay figures which are specially treated with fluorescent paint. The result is magnificent. There are seventeen pieces in that scene and it cost £1,000 to create … The Merry Dell animal kingdom … This is a piece of another world, the world a child might imagine in a dream.'

The Roker End of Roker Park football ground during the World Cup in July 1966. Italy, Chile, USSR and Hungary played at Roker Park in the World Cup games. Italian supporters are in the car on the right. Another extraordinary event took place at the Roker Park ground in June 1987 when David Bowie performed in front of 36,000 fans. Bowie's Glass Spider Tour was the biggest rock event in Wearside's history.

Three
Seaburn

Sea Lane ... Tentland ... Bent's Farm ... Corporation's
Ambitions ... Bellerby's Amusements ... Guidi's ...
H.M.S. Sentinel ... Seaburn Camp ...

Seaburn tram terminus, c. 1935. The tram on the right, No. 61, was a curiosity which was built in 1920 as an open topped car. No. 61 was modernised in 1934 and a cover was constructed to house half of the twenty-eight upper deck passengers. The new 'turret car' was an experiment and if it proved a popular design there were plans to similarly alter other cars. However, tram No. 61 became known as the 'Ice Box' among Wearsiders and it remained a unique experience. Access to and from the seafront for the vast majority was by walking or by tramcar. On August Bank Holiday 1948 the queue at the tram terminus of families returning home stretched for half a mile.

The 'better off' arrived in other forms of transport.

Sea Lane, *c.* 1910, before the area became more commonly known as Seaburn. The narrow road to Whitburn, short promenade and the beach in the foreground were controlled by Sunderland Rural District Council. The land and beach further along the promenade were also outside of Sunderland Borough Council's jurisdiction. South Shields Rural District Council were responsible for what was considered to be the best stretch of golden sands on this part of the North East coast.

Sea Lane showing signs of development, *c.* 1910. At the far end of the promenade a cafe has been built. Seaburn Cafe is the large building on the left. In the background on the right is Bent's Farm, perched on 'Whitburn Banks'.

The beach at Whitburn Bay, *c.* 1910. The road system to Seaburn needed improving first before any further developments could be successful. In 1923 South Shields Rural District Council set about improving access from the north by employing workless ex-servicemen to straighten, widen and make a better quality road from the Jolly Sailor pub to Sunderland Rural District Council's boundary at Seaburn. The improvements included removing the gasometer at the Fishermen's Cottages and raising the unsafe dip in the road on the north side of Seaburn Camp.

A postcard scene of Sea Lane, *c.* 1919. Seats have been constructed with the new promenade and more buildings have been added at the far end. An inscription in this area read: 'This Sea Wall and Promenade was constructed for the Rural District Council of Sunderland by Henry Bell, contractor of Ryhope, and dedicated on their behalf to the public on 13 August 1918, by William Fawcett, JP, Chairman.'

The scene, at the north end of the promenade near 'Whitburn Banks', on the same day as the previous photograph. At the Sunderland Police dinner in 1923, Chief Superintendent Ruddick said: 'South Shields is coming very fast southwards and I have not the slightest doubt that within the next few years, if Sunderland Corporation have not extended in their direction, they will find themselves left at Sea Lane, where they are now.'

H.M.S. *Sentinel* grounded at the north end of Seaburn in 1923. Notice the absence of a promenade on the left. On 13 February 1923 the cruiser was being towed to Thomas Young's scrapyard at the South Dock for breaking up when she broke away. *Sentinel* went ashore at Seaburn and was scuttled to avoid further danger. Record crowds visited Seaburn on Sunday afternoon 18 March and watched four tugs make another unsuccessful attempt to move the war vessel. Thousands of people had either walked to the seafront or arrived in packed tramcars to see the unusual spectacle. Tramcar receipts for the day amounted to £296 which was £102 above the corresponding week in 1922. Each failure to re-float *Sentinel* meant a month long wait for an exceptional high tide. H.M.S. *Sentinel* was finally pulled off the shore on 18 June 1923, perhaps to the disappointment of the tramways company, local traders and hawkers who had done good business from the large crowds.

Tents and deck chairs could be hired from this building at the north end of Seaburn promenade in the 1920s. Further along the prom is Just's Cafe. Around 1930 tent hire prices soared and private hire companies were accused of exploiting the public. *The Sunderland Echo* called for the Corporation to take over the tent hiring to end the monopoly. The council discussed the matter and private hire companies complained that their livelihoods were threatened by proposals to make it a municipal concern. In 1934 the Corporation took control of the beaches and purchased three hundred tents and two thousand chairs. Prices were fixed: hire of bathing cabins, threepence per person (child twopence); hire of towel, one penny; hire of costumes, one penny; hire of helmets, twopence; chairs, twopence per session; tents, two shillings, and two shillings and sixpence on August Bank Holiday. A season ticket for a tent cost five shillings.

Tentland at Seaburn in the 1920s. Several designs of tent can be seen, many were privately owned. In 1934 the Corporation charged sixpence for placing private tents on the beach.

Bent's Farm shortly before it was demolished, c. 1930, so that Sunderland could make a new seafront road. The inclusion of Fulwell in the Borough boundaries in 1928 opened up new and exciting possibilities for development of the seafront. The relatively flat farmlands near Sea Lane, the burn running through the dene to the sea at Whitburn Bay; as well as the extensive golden beach anciently known as Fulwell Sands, provided acres for potential development, and an alternative to the rocks and cliffs of Roker. But before Sunderland could realise its ambition to become the leading North East coast resort. '… one of the first obstacles to be overcome is the sewerage problem which has for long been a bugbear to all interested in the possibilities of Sunderland's seafront,' said the Mayor, Dr I. G. Modlin in September 1930. Sewage from outlets at Whitburn Steel, Whitburn Bay and the Holey Rock was regularly washed up on the beaches, and Dr Modlin felt the priority was to deal with the sewers first before spending thousands of pounds developing the resorts.

An unusual view of Seaburn beach, c. 1930. Seaburn Cafe, on the left, was demolished shortly afterwards, to provide space for the new seafront road. Just to the right of the cafe are terraced houses, the gable end of which became Hastings' post office.

An interesting aerial view of Seaburn in 1932 which shows open spaces ready for leisure development, and, of course, for housing which has begun. Seaburn Cafe on the corner has been demolished and the seafront road has been widened. A small fairground can be seen where the Seaburn Hotel and a shopping complex will be built. In late September 1930 Roker Development Committee approved ambitious plans for Roker and Seaburn and asked the Corporation to sanction the scheme. At Roker there were proposals for: improvement of the lower promenade between Holey Rock and the pier; and eight shelters for Cliff Park. The principle part of the scheme, however, was from Seaburn tram terminus along to the Borough boundary at Whitburn. There were plans for: a shopping centre; hotel and kinema; amusement park and pleasure gardens; a concert hall and bandstand; as well as a children's paddling pool and small bungalows with terraces for sunbathing for holiday makers. Sunderland Rent and Ratepayers' Association strongly opposed the scheme, and 'moderates' on the council condemned it as 'extravagant' in a period of grave economic problems. 'We do not want fancy picture halls and dance halls,' said Councillor C. W. Fryers. 'If that is to be done let it be done by private enterprise.' There was discontent at the council's policy of attracting visitors from all parts of the North East. A Seaburn tradesman commented in September 1930: 'We do not want to attract large crowds of day-trippers who bring little or no advantage to the town at the expense of our own townspeople who are not able to enjoy the seaside amenities to the same extent as before. The other day I saw twelve charabanc trips come into Seaburn. They all had food and drink with them. They spent the day on the beach and probably never spent a penny with a Sunderland shopkeeper.' The depression of the early 1930s continued to hinder the development of Seaburn. Plans were revised and schemes deferred. In January 1935 the Corporation announced a plan to borrow £25,000 to construct an open air swimming pool at Seaburn, and plans for a new dance hall were dispatched to the Ministry of Health, but both schemes were turned down. Meanwhile, the council were dealing with the Holey Rock problem. (See pp. 15-17.)

Seaburn in the 1930s. The far end of the promenade has been extended to Whitburn and the Corporation have built a shelter into Whitburn Banks. However, the hut that can be seen on the promenade has disappeared on the photograph below.

A postcard scene of Seaburn looking north from Roker in the 1930s. The Corporation shelter can be seen on the extreme right. Shops and cafes have been built. This postcard is postmarked 7 September 1938: 'Dear mother and sisters, I am spending an enjoyable holiday over here. The weather is perfect. Have spent today here. It is a most lovely place. Hope mother is keeping nicely. Love to you all, Clara.'

PROPOSED DEVELOP[ ]

SEABURN

Another plan put forward by the Seaside Development and Entertainment Committee was approved by the council in February 1936. Key: 1. Sea water swimming pool near the shelter and to be constructed on Parson's Rocks; 2. Hotel; 3. Paddling pool; 4. Boating lake; 5. Golf course; 6. Car park; 7. Gardens; 8 and 9. Tennis courts and bowling green; 10. Concert hall; 11. Dykelands Road. The scheme was more realistic that previous ambitions and many of the features reached fruition. During the prosperity of the late 1930s the golf course, which was opened in 1930 on the Burn Field, was converted to a boating pool, and a new nine hole golf course was laid out. A new hotel was built (see p. 57) as well as a modern dance hall (see p. 58), but the war put a halt to further progress, and plans for the swimming pool, tennis courts and bowling green never materialised.

An advertisement from the late 1930s. Prior to the First World War Leonello Guidi (pronounced Gweedy) opened a fish and chip shop in a village near Kilmarnock. Leonello was escaping the poverty in Barga, a small village in Tuscany, Italy. After the war there was a move south to County Durham and Leonello opened an ice cream parlour in Silksworth Row, Sunderland. The business expanded and in the early 1920s Guidi's opened another shop in a wooden hut on the lower promenade at Roker. From 1933 the family traded from a purpose built cafeteria in Queen's Parade, Seaburn called the Popular Cafe. After Leonello's death in the late 1930s his eldest child Evelyn took sole control of the business. Eighty-nine-year-old Evelyn remembers: 'During the Second World War our cafe was popular with soldiers billeted at the Drill Hall round the corner in Dykelands Road. One day an officer came to the cafe and asked me to open up on Christmas Day for his soldiers who were shortly to leave for the war. I agreed and they supplied the food which we cooked and served to them. It was to be their last Christmas dinner because we received news that their ship had been sunk and the soldiers were lost at sea. It was very sad.' (See also pp. 64 & 69.)

The Central Café of the Front
EXCELLENT SERVICE AND CUISINE.

GUIDIS
POPULAR CAFE
SEABURN
Special Terms to
PRIVATE AND PLEASURE PARTIES

Bellerby's amusements at Seaburn in the late 1920s. Roker Pier and Lighthouse are in the background. Bellerby's owned rides and amusements at Seaburn from the 1920s up to the mid 1980s when they moved to Roker. The Bellerby family currently occupy Roker Amusement Arcade on the lower promenade.

A close up of the roundabout shown on the upper photograph. Edward Bellerby jnr is on the left. This small children's ride was hand operated by gearing near to the centre pole. When Sunderland Corporation wanted the attractions moved to the permanent site on the south side of the new Whitburn Road in the late 1930s, E. W. Bellerby snr wasn't happy about the move, and the family took their amusements to South Shields. However, they returned to Seaburn after an absence of one year and set up their amusements on the new site next to where Seaburn Hall would be built.

An early and unfamiliar scene of Seaburn Camp, *c.* 1912. Many people remember the black blocks of military huts at Seaburn Camp which were utilised by the Corporation for residential educational visits by school children. The huts were also used as changing rooms by school and local football teams. In June 1976 caretaker Peter Boyle discovered some old documents while he was demolishing some panelling in one of the buildings which was formerly the guardroom. The papers belonged to the 3rd Battalion Sherwood Foresters who had been stationed at Seaburn Camp during the First World War. Most of the records related to charges made against soldiers caught on Sunderland Railway Station without passes. The find also revealed that 427 men were stationed at the Camp in 1918.

Two scenes of children on holiday at Seaburn Camp in July 1929. Above: Games taking place on the recreation field. Below: Exercises on the beach. Seaburn Camp became a children's holiday camp in 1920. The facility allowed four hundred children to take a holiday over the summer period.

Seaburn Hotel in 1965. In line with the policy to develop the seafront, Sunderland Corporation leased land at the corner of Seaburn Terrace and Whitburn Road for the purpose of building an 'up market' hotel. Plans drawn up by the architect Mr T. R. Milburn were passed by the council in March 1936. A four million pound revamp began in December 1989 when the building was practically demolished and rebuilt. The name was changed to the Swallow Hotel.

Former Sunderland Football Club favourite and skipper, Charlie Hurley signs an autograph in the Seaburn Hotel in February 1973. Charlie returned to Wearside as manager of Reading for an FA Cup fourth round tie against his old club. Charlie received a tremendous reception from the 33,000 crowd at Roker Park. The result was 1-1 draw. Sunderland won the replay 3-1 and of course went on to win the cup in May 1973.

Seaburn Hall in the mid 1950s. A plan produced in November 1934 by Mr O. H. Mark, the council architect, for a concert and dance hall costing £29,000 was approved by the Seaside Development and Entertainment Committee of the Corporation. However, a modified scheme costing £13,696 was passed by the council in September 1938, and the foundation stone was laid on 16 March 1939. Seaburn Hall was officially opened on 28 July 1939 by Councillor W. A. Bell, Chairman of the Seaside Development Committee. The building not only became popular for dances but local and national conferences were held there. On 13 November 1951 *Wot Cheor Geordie!* was broadcast for the Home Service from Seaburn Hall. Star of the show was forty-year-old, up and coming comedian, Bobby Thompson. Bobby was employed as an assembler at a Royal Ordnance factory at Birtley and he was making his third appearance on the show. Seaburn Hall had been host to another BBC radio show when in June 1948 *Up and Doing* was broadcast. The programme starred comedian Tony Astor, Clive Wayne, and The Banjoliers. Richard Kelly produced the show. In the 1970s Seaburn Hall housed the Beer Kellar and when the Collins' Ocean Park complex failed, the building deteriorated, was vandalised and became an eyesore. Seaburn Hall became a danger to the public and was demolished in July 1982. There was sadness and anger that a well known amenity for the people of Sunderland had disappeared and the council were criticised for allowing the building to fall into ruin.

A collage of singers and bands at Seaburn Hall used in a 1950s advertisement.

Four
Seaburn After the War

Beaches Opened Again … 'Master Plan' … Sunspot of the North East … Modest Developments … Huge Crowds … Lost Children … Failure and Decline … Boxing Day Dip …

As part of the 'Holidays at Home' scheme during the Second World War the beach was opened at Seaburn for the August Bank Holiday weekend in 1944. The photograph shows that every available place is occupied by family groups, many of whom arrived early to claim a good spot. Notice the absence of deck chairs. There was an exciting holiday atmosphere present among Wearsiders deprived of the beaches for almost five years. The seaside crowds were boosted by large numbers of evacuees from London who were living on Wearside to escape the flying bombs.

Children at Seaburn over the August Bank Holiday weekend, 1944. For many of them playing on the sand and plodging in the sea was a new experience. *The Echo* reported that the children went mad with delight at Seaburn beach. One elderly Wearsider commented: 'It does your heart good to see them.'

PROMENADE AND BEACH, SEABURN, SUNDERLAND.

The seafront in the late 1940s. In March 1945 Sunderland beaches were finally opened to the public permanently when the Army began removing barbed wire, scaffolding and other obstacles. The public were warned of the dangers and that they entered the beaches at their own risk. The authorities emphasised that no one should pick up unusual objects brought in by the tide. The war had interrupted progress on the development of Seaburn, but in September 1946 the Seaside Development and Entertainment Committee produced a one million pound 'master plan' for consideration by the council. The aim of the scheme was to turn Seaburn and Roker into a leading British seaside resort and the entertainment centre of the North East coast. The master plan included a large theatre accommodating 3,000 people and designed to be the best in the North of England; a children's theatre to seat 500; an arena for indoor circuses; and the laying out of Cliff Park with flower beds, tennis courts and bowling greens. Unfortunately, post war recovery was slow and none of the facilities materialised. The Corporation saw the future success of Seaburn by promoting a balance of municipal and privately run facilities. In January 1951 they made known their ambition to turn Seaburn and Roker into one of the top four seaside resorts in Britain, and the revised master plan included: constructing a short pier at Seaburn on which there would be catering facilities and other amenities; an open air swimming pool - a revival of 1930s plans; a caravan site; and a traffic free seafront. Once again the economic situation prevented action and the master plan was frozen. Nonetheless, the thousands of visitors to Seaburn after the war justified the need for more attractions. The Corporation were trying to develop a resort without any real facilities and most of the erections were restricted to temporary huts and tents. There were some modest developments, however, when in 1950 a private company erected a roller skating rink near to Dykelands Road, and next to it a council run cafeteria opened in 1951. Although an offer to bring a zoo to Seaburn in 1950 was turned down by the council. Meanwhile, in May 1948 the Corporation had trebled Seaburn Amusement rates which was 'a shattering blow to Seaburn,' said William Jackson the Corporation's Entertainment manager, who was trying to attract more private enterprise to the seafront. Despite this setback, Seaburn fairground proprietor William Noble signed a four year lease agreement. Other attractions boosted the seafront crowds, like the annual Roker Regatta, and in August 1947 the Durham County Agricultural Show held its centenary meeting at Seaburn. On the opening Saturday more that 18,000 people had paid to enter the showground. During the summer of 1947 the Seaside Entertainment Department made a profit of £2,689 in the municipal venture. In November 1949 the Ministry of Food classified Seaburn and Roker as an official resort. The recognition was important and was mainly due to the efforts of Sunderland Confectioners' Association. Rationing was still in force, and the listing as an official resort meant that during the summer of 1950 seafront tradesmen received an additional allocation of sweets to meet the demands of holiday crowds.

Crowds near the boating pool and fair in 1948. Seaburn Follies is on the right where entertainers performed. The wooden structure was burnt down in November 1948. The figures recorded from council run seafront amenities provide evidence of the huge influx of visitors for the season April to October 1950: 98,642 used the boating pool; 166,310 borrowed deck chairs; 23,599 played on the golf course; 46,782 children and 39,728 adults rode on the miniature railway; 18,443 tents were hired; 17,043 meals were served - the favourite being fish and chips. These numbers were in spite of a poor summer in 1950, compared to the heat-wave of 1949.

The front cover of Sunderland Corporation's 1954 Guide to Roker and Seaburn. In the early 1950s the council started a campaign to advertise Sunderland's seaside resorts at railway stations throughout the North of England. The importance of advertising to attract visitors other than Wearsiders to the seafront was known in the 1930s. However, the authors of the 1913 Sunderland Year Book described Roker as 'The Brighton of Sunderland', and, 'Sunderland has spent many thousands of pounds on Roker, and without doubt it is now one of the finest watering places on the North East coast. But it wants advertising, and the Town Council extravagant in some things, are niggardly in this, to their loss be it said' ... Roker is popular enough with the people of Sunderland, and would be so with holiday makers from a distance if its many attractions were made known.'

Seaburn fairground next to Seaburn Hall in the late 1940s. Bellerby's children's wheel ride is in the foreground and Noble's octopus ride is behind. To accommodate the first stage of a new five year scheme to improve Seaburn, the fairground had to be moved back from Whitburn Road in 1954. Noble's were against moving to the new site and decided to quit Seaburn for a move to South Shields.

William Noble's amusements are auctioned in March 1954. An air raid siren is perched on Seaburn Hall on the right. The fair was moved back and work began to build several kiosks, picnic and play areas, and an exhibition lawn and flower beds between Seaburn Hall and the boating pool. A paved access from Whitburn Road to the fairground completed the scheme at a cost of £21,637.

The entrance to the fairground in May 1955. The Collins family took over from Noble's in 1954 as the leading tenant on Seaburn fair. They brought with them the Big Dipper which was a replica of the dipper at Battersea Park, London. The fair is shown after it was set back from Whitburn Road as part of Sunderland Corporation's development scheme. The Big Dipper can be seen in the background. When the Corporation decided to move the fair, a site was initially chosen next to Seaburn Camp until it was pointed out that the fair would have a 'detrimental effect' on the school children resident there.

Ann Arkle, aged 12, (right) on the roller skating rink at Seaburn in 1953. Ann spent most of her spare time on the rink which opened in 1950 and she remembers: 'The rink was open air with a rail barrier around it. There was no roof and when it rained puddles formed. The rink was closed in winter, but because it was open air children climbed the barrier to use it. In about 1954 the roller skating rink moved to South Shields and I used to travel on my bike to skate on it.' Ann later worked in the Popular Cafe at Seaburn owned by her mother Evelyn Arkle (nee Guidi). A unique feature of the interior of the Popular Cafe, remembered by many Wearsiders, was the beautiful embroidery which lined the walls. 'They were all made by my mother,' said Ann, 'and the framed works were admired by our customers.' (See also pp. 54 & 69.)

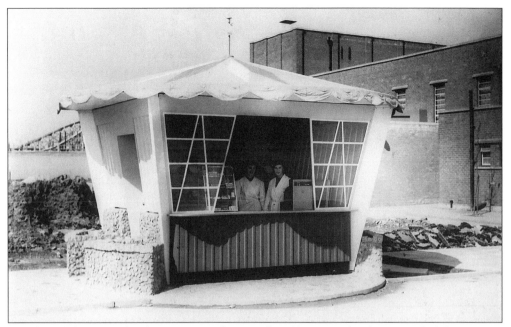

The first of the 'super kiosks' was opened in April 1955 in time for the Easter holidays. Seven more kiosks were completed for the Spring holiday in 1955 as part of the first stage of the Seaburn development scheme. One of the kiosks sold toffee apples, another fish food with willicks a 'tanner' (2½p) a bag with a pin, and another sold candy floss.

Seaburn, *c.* 1960, showing the super kiosks, lawns and flower beds which created an attractive seafront. Billy Bellerby remembers that Gypsy Rose Lee, the fortune teller, had one of the kiosks for her business: 'In the late 1960s there were break-ins and she wanted to buy our pet dog to guard her kiosk. My father said to her, 'What do you need a dog for? You can see into the future can't you? You'll know when they are going to break in, so phone the police!'

Teenagers Judith Atkinson (left), now Balzi, and her cousin Brenda Cripps, now Simes, enjoying candy floss at Seaburn, c. 1959. The girls are wearing rock n' roll flared skirts. The cousins are good friends and they were evacuated together from Hendon to St John's Chapel in 1943 when they were about two-years-old. Judith recalls that in the late 1940s and early '50s much of her leisure time as a child was spent on Hendon beach, but sometimes they would go to Roker and travel on the ferry from the East End to Monkwearmouth.

The circus came to Seaburn in 1977 and one of the stars took a dip in the sea.

The fairground and adjacent picnic area and kiosks in the early 1960s. In the bottom right corner is Billy Kaye's Prize Bingo. Above the bingo is 'The Hurricane', an exciting ride imported from Germany. Bellerby's rides border the perimeter fence from the entrance with the two towers to Collins' Amusement Arcade on the left.

The entertainment area of Seaburn in 1961. On the right, next to Dykelands Road, is the miniature railway track (see pp. 4 & 93). Two bridges crossed the burn which fed water into the boating pool. Underground pipes at the other end of the pool carried an overflow to the sea. On Whitburn Road, near to the corner of Dykelands Road, is the underground toilet block where visitors could get a 'wash and brush up' for threepence. The impressive Big Dipper highlights the fair which backed onto the nine hole miniature golf course. A children's ride of a swan leading ducklings toured the inside of the Big Dipper passing by cartoon character figures. On the beach side of the fair is Seaburn Hall.

Seaburn in the early 1950s. Post war crowds were boosted by Scots. In 1950 employees of Corporation run amenities took over two hundred Scottish banknotes in one week. This postcard is postmarked 16 July 1957. To: Mrs A. Rully, 4 Cairnban Street, Glasgow, SW1. 'Dear Mum, Have had a nice time here. The people seem to be very fond of Scotsmen. Weather has been rainy but not enough to hold back the merriments. Give my love to Pop and the gang. Lots of love, Jock.'

An advertisement from the Borough of Sunderland's 1962 Guide to Roker and Seaburn. In 1958 the Corporation introduced a scheme for cut rate holidays at the twin resorts for pensioners. Sunderland joined a list of other British resorts who ran a 'pensioners season' in June and September. British Railways joined in the scheme by reducing fares for block bookings of old folk. Several of the seafront boarding houses agreed to reduce their rates, but it was acknowledged that hotel accommodation was scarce in Sunderland and continued to be a problem.

Seaburn in 1963 shows the result of 1930s and 1950s developments which turned the area into a popular and busy holiday resort. Guidi's Popular Cafe in Queen's Parade opened in 1933 and the family were in business there until the early 1960s. The family also sold takeaway fish and chips and hot water from a window at the rear of the cafe. Ann Hughes (nee Arkle) remembers: 'We were kept busy by the crowds that visited Seaburn in the 1950s and early '60s. I can remember the large queues waiting for buses in Dykelands Road in the late afternoon and early evening. They extended up the back lane and past our hatch window. The aroma of our freshly fried fish and chips must have been too much to resist and we served until the bus queues disappeared.' Ann and her mother Evelyn remember the stars who visited the Popular Cafe in the 1950s and early '60s: Frankie Vaughan, Jimmy Young, Tommy Steele, Marty Wilde, Ronnie Hilton and Frankie Howard. They were appearing at the Empire and were probably staying at the Seaburn Hotel. The cafe is now occupied by the Shagorika Indian Restaurant. (See also pp. 54 & 64.)

The Leamington family on Seaburn beach during the 1967 Spring Holiday. Suits are still in fashion for the beach. Notice the man sitting near the steps wearing a tie.

A family on Seaburn beach in August 1967.

A pony and cart ride on Seaburn beach in the 1950s.

Seaburn beach in 1976. Remember the long hot, dry summer of 1976 when the grass turned brown and the highest July temperatures were recorded on Wearside for forty-three years? Temperatures at Sunderland had soared to the 80s in June 1976 and were higher than Madrid, Barcelona and Majorca. Numerous cases of sun burn were treated at the Royal Infirmary and a doctor recommended a pint of beer and a bag of crisps as a way of 'cooling it' and to take in more salt. *The Sunderland Echo* reported on the 28 June 1976 that all roads to the beach were full and the tar was melting causing cars to skid.

Four-year-old Kevin Todd of Cobham Square, Southwick has been collected from the Lost Children and First Aid Station by his mother Mrs Janet Todd in August 1977. An announcement over the public address system that a child had been found was followed by a description and often the wailing of the distraught child was heard in the background.

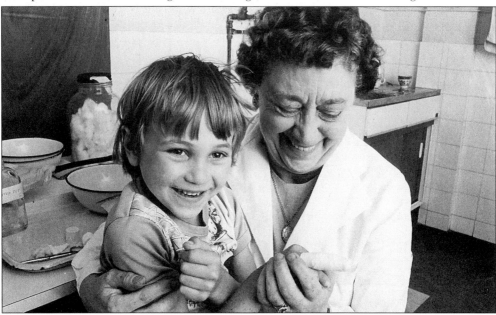

First aid attendant Mrs Betty Hagel treating seven-year-old Malcolm Passmore of North View, North Lambton in August 1977. Malcolm had jammed his finger in the door of the gents. The season from April to October 1950 revealed the following statistics at the busy resorts of Seaburn and Roker: 750 lost children were dealt with. The facility was free but parents could give a voluntary donation of threepence to provide toys for other lost children. There were 1,758 first aid casualties, which included five dog bites, one donkey bite, fifteen jelly fish stings, five people were kicked by donkeys and ninety-eight people had sand cleared from their eyes.

Dolphins arrive at Sea World's Dolphinarium, *c.* 1973. In the early 1970s P. & J. Collins, the fairground family, were granted a thirty-five year lease for land at Seaburn which included Ocean Park Fairground, Seaburn Hall and the area south to Dykelands Road. In October 1972 ambitious plans were submitted to the council by the Collins brothers which included the construction of a Sea World on the site of the Golf Club. Despite strong moral objections to bringing intelligent dolphins to Sunderland to perform tricks, the development scheme at Seaburn went ahead. The 1970s however, saw the decline of Seaburn as a resort. Seafront trade suffered as holiday habits changed and many Wearside families travelled abroad for the sun, and to escape the vagaries of North East coast weather. The 1976 heat wave had attracted crowds to the seafront but summer 1977 was a washout. By the end of July 1978 another summer was passing by and seafront trade was poor. Seaburn's decline came to a head in August 1978 when the Collins' business crashed with debts of £152,000. This figure included £58,000 owed to the council for three years rent and rates. The council took over the amusements complex, but there wasn't the money available for development. Meanwhile the council looked for a private concern to manage the area. Criticisms were aimed at the council for allowing the run down of Seaburn as a resort and that Seaburn Hall could have been put to better use. The fairground was shabby and forlorn, and in August 1979 *The Echo* wrote: 'Only a creak of a broken gate at the entrance to the fairground and the wind whistling through empty buildings disturbed the silence.' The general appearance of the seafront 'lacked civic pride,' wrote Canon J. G. Bates the Vicar of St Andrew's in the parish magazine '... Grass ill kept and badly cut. Edges untrimmed and weeds all over the place ... Broken railings and seats in need of repair ... There is a refusal to make the most of what we have and put the town on show.' Indeed, there seemed to prevail an attitude that the seafront is there - take it or leave it! So ended an unhappy decade for Seaburn and Roker and the future of the twin resorts was undoubtedly uncertain. However, despite the problems the ailing resorts were clearly recognised by the Northumbrian Tourist Board in November 1979 which saw 'considerable tourist potential' in the area. They went on to say that there was a need of an official Tourist Information Centre in Sunderland.

The Boxing Day Dip in the early 1990s. The popular annual event attracts several hundred sponsored dippers. It is cleverly organised by The Lions Club of Sunderland and the first dip took place in 1976 when forty people raised £450. The number of dippers peaked to 845 in 1990, and in 1996 almost £20,000 was raised for charity. The Boxing Day Dip has grown into the biggest of its kind in Europe.

'Seaburn Centre Keep Fit' won first prize as the best women's team in the 1994 Boxing Day Dip. The team entered as 'Old Mother Hubbard and Her Children'. Pictured are four of the 'children'. Left to right: Pat O'Brien, Margaret Waugh, Dorothy O'Neill and Andrea Bruce. The Mayor and his wife help to judge the fancy dress competition before leading the dippers in a procession to the beach, where two to three thousand spectators were entertained as the hardy dippers enter the sea.

A series of three photographs taken by Dick Cook in the late 1970s which capture the fascination of rough seas at Seaburn.

Youths play the dangerous game of 'dodging the waves' as the white water smashes up the steps and over the sea wall.

Two lads are almost engulfed by the sea.

This familiar scene recorded in 1989 illustrates how quickly changes take place. The Seaburn Hotel is about to undergo a four million pound revamp and a name change to The Swallow Hotel. Then, of course, is the controversial fountain which has an uncertain future. The

terraced houses on the left have been demolished to make way for another hotel extension, but Seaburn Post Office was left standing on its own. Alex Hastings, the former Sunderland footballer and captain, ran the post office and newsagent business in the 1930s. In 1948 Ron Wood and his wife Joan took over but the shop was still known as 'Hastings'. Hastings was a well known landmark at Seaburn terminus where last minute films for cameras, buckets and spades, beach balls, cricket sets, windmills and floaters were bought before a visit to the beach. Mr and Mrs Wood retired in June 1977 after running Hastings for twenty-nine years. The Woods said that they had the satisfaction of being part of the community at Seaburn. 'We have sold comics and toys to the children of the children we knew when we took over the shop. We have seen families grow up in the area,' said Mr Wood.

Seaburn Post Office in May 1997.

Five

Our Entertainment

Jumbo ... 1950s Illuminations ... Big Top ... Village Queen ... The Fair ... Big Dipper ... Sand Artists ... Bonnie Prince Charlie ...

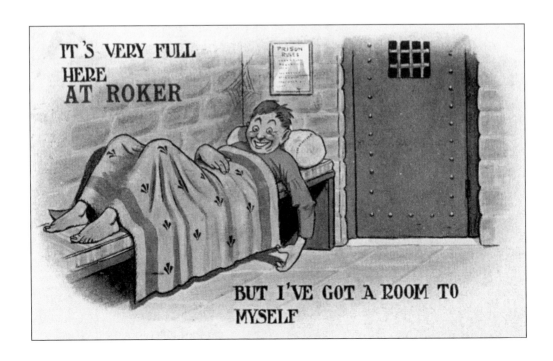

The elephant ride at Seaburn in 1949. 'Jumbo's' operator, Jimmy Sawyer, controlled the petrol engine powered machine by a lever behind its ear. 'Our family and several other families used to gather on the beach opposite Seaburn Camp for a day out in the late 1940s, and I can remember the elephant ride very clearly,' recalls Mrs Sheila Smith. 'To us children in those days the elephant was fascinating. We hadn't seen anything like it before. It was so realistic and a ride on it was a real treat. There were queues for a ride opposite the Seaburn Camp entrance on the beach side of the road. It was exciting for a small child and Jimmy Sawyer was a nice man who made a lot of children happy.'

John Usher and his grandson Tommy Davis on Seaburn promenade in July 1951. Notice the steps behind them which led to the seats on the mechanical elephant. The name Jumbo can be seen on the arch.

In June 1950 electricians are preparing set pieces for the Roker and Seaburn illuminations. The lights had been restored to the seafront in 1949 after a gap of eleven years caused by the war and slow post war recovery. The revived lights were on a much smaller scale compared to the 1930s illuminations because of financial restrictions and a fire which had destroyed many of the stored set pieces. At the opening night of 3 September 1949 unprecedented crowds made their way to the seafront and took the organisers by surprise. There was traffic congestion and chaos but about 100,000 people were present for the forty-five minute fireworks display and official switch on for the month long illuminations. Emergency plans succeeded in coping with the crowds and traffic for the following weekend when 300 coaches arrived from many parts of the North of England.

The Roker Park keeper's house illuminated during the early 1950s.

The entry gate to Roker Park for the 1952 illuminations. Adults admitted for one shilling and children for sixpence. Some extraordinary sales figures were produced for the second Saturday night of the illuminations in September 1949. At Seaburn 1,800 people travelled on the miniature railway; 700 on the boating pool; 5,486 ice creams were sold, as well as 600 bags of chips and 4,000 bags of potato crisps. The Illuminations Committee were aware of competition from neighbouring resorts and made the 1950 illuminations 'bigger and brighter'. The 'Fairy Dell' made a return for the first time since before the war.

A set piece in Roker Park as part of the illuminations during the early 1950s is pictured at day and night. By the end of 1953 the illuminations had made a loss of £20,813 since they began in 1949 and there were complaints that ratepayers were footing the bill. Inflation fuelled resentment when the rate was increased from 16s 8d (83p) in the pound in 1951 to 23s 2d (£1.16) by 1953 - the highest rate in the Town's history.

Roker Park bandstand during the 1950s illuminations. Entertainers are on a temporary stage below the bandstand where there is an accompanying band. Provoked by the cost of the illuminations and the increased rate, a 'Battle of the Lights' began in about September 1953 and an 'Anti-Illuminations Group' was formed. In June 1954 a petition of 24,000 names, which backed the campaign against the lights, was handed to the Mayor. The general feeling was that the lights were an extremely good attraction but a leader of the group Mr Bethel said: 'Let there be light but in the right places in the houses still inflicted with low pressure gas and in poorly illuminated streets.' The cost of the seafront illuminations couldn't be justified and although there was an initial three years ban the lights didn't appear again. In 1959 the illuminations were sold off.

The performers and band taken at about the same time as the previous photograph.

Entertainment or cruelty? Lion taming at a circus at Seaburn, *c.* 1950. There were strong protests by animal rights activists in May 1989 when Chipperfield's Circus arrived at Seaburn Recreation Ground for a two week stay. Fake cancellation notices were stuck on posters advertising the circus and anti-circus protest leader Councillor Uta Clay said: 'There is a place for circuses providing employment and good entertainment, but it doesn't have to be at the cost of utterly miserable lives of animals.' From 1 January 1990 Sunderland Council banned all circuses from the town which featured wild animals.

Six elephants weighing two tons each created an unusual scene in Roker Avenue in October 1947. The elephants had arrived at Monkwearmouth Railway Station and were on their way to Seaburn to form part of Bertram Mills Circus. The big top was erected on Seaburn car park to provide thrills for 3,500 spectators.

The boating lake and fairground, c. 1960. The Big Dipper was a well known landmark which dominated the skyline at Seaburn Fairground for about fifteen years. It is remembered as the most daring and exciting ride on the fair. The highlight of the ride was the anticipation of the slow climb to the 'hump' about fifty feet above the ground. The five car train then sharply descended causing 'butterflies' in stomachs and squeals from girls. One day in July 1967 about twenty people were riding in the train when the wire rope, which pulled the cars to the top of the hump, slipped from its attachment. The train continued on over the hump and plummeted out of control down the steep slope. Three of the cars derailed and seven injured people were taken to hospital. The end of the Big Dipper came on a Sunday afternoon in June 1970. The leading car suddenly left the track throwing out four passengers. A fifteen-year-old boy from Ryhope was killed when he was flung thirty feet to the ground. The Big Dipper closed after the fatal accident and wasn't used again. The demolition was completed in February 1973. It had taken several months to level the structure.

The train descends the hump on the Big Dipper in 1960.

Seaburn in the early 1950s. In the background is the popular pleasure boat *The Village Queen*.

The Village Queen, in the early 1950s, was owned by Ralph Ray of Whitburn. The open pleasure boat was a converted lifeboat and could carry ten passengers. Wooden gantries on wheels were pushed in and out to suit the tide and provided access to the boat. The Ray brothers were fishermen and six of them worked on *The Village Queen* at various times. Albert Ray played the accordion on the gantry steps to attract customers. The Rays worked *The Village Queen* from the Whitburn side of the Borough boundary and applied to Boldon Council for day licenses. The arrangement was convenient because trade depended on the weather.

The Ray family, around 1950. Left to right: Ann and husband Ralph who owned *The Village Queen*; Hilda and husband Albert; and Emily Ray. Two friends are kneeling at the front. In the background *The Village Queen* is standing off, and the gangway on wheels can be seen.

The Sea Spray pleasure boat plied from opposite the Seaburn Hotel and provided another 'in and out' journey. James Ridley of Elmwood Avenue, Southwick owned *The Sea Spray* in the 1950s. He was the father-in-law of Ralph Ray owner of *The Village Queen*. James Ridley obtained a seasonal license from Sunderland Corporation.

Bellerby's fairground in the late 1920s. The 'Aerial Cars' also known as the 'Shuggy Boats' are on the left. The family owned these rides until about 1980 when they were smashed up. E. W. Bellerby jnr is the man standing beside the roundabout. On the right, two boys are sitting on horses which are probably intended for assembly on the centre pole on the extreme left of the upper picture on p. 55.

On the left is E. W. Bellerby snr, and on the right is his partner Samuel Adam. The occasion was the arrival of a new specially made roundabout in the 1950s which both men proudly display.

Bellerby's 'super-cars' and oval shaped track with pay box on the centre island, in the late 1940s. The cars were petrol powered and a whistle was blown when time was up, but sometimes it was necessary for an attendant to jump on the rear bumper to pull a lever which stopped the engine when a driver refused to stop. The shuggy boats are in the background, and further back is Seaburn Hall. On the left is Bellerby's Wonderland Penny Arcade.

Fairground scene looking south towards Dykelands Road in the mid to late 1950s. The shuggy boats which travelled with Bellerby's from site to site are on the left. In the centre is an old style roundabout with no platform. On the right is the 'Mickey Mouse Ride', so called because it was covered with Disney characters. Later, these rides were moved to another part of the fairground to provide space for P. & J. Collins' Amusement Arcade. Many people will remember the arcade which was on the left to the entrance of the fair.

Edward William Bellerby snr, who started the family fairground business, with 'Dobbies' ride in about 1960. After First World War service, Edward opened a small business hiring out bicycles in the Southwick area. He then bought some fairground rides and travelled from site to site in a caravan before he established himself at Seaburn.

Another fairground scene in the 1950s taken on the same day as the lower photograph on p. 87. The Helter Skelter is on the extreme left. On the right is the Big Dipper pay box. Next to the pay box, on the left, is the roundabout shown on the lower photograph on p. 86.

The dodgem cars, c. 1960. They were popular rides and a meeting place for teenagers who would sit on the barrier to listen to the latest hits and watch the dodgems. The pay box is on the left. For one person hiring a car was a shilling, or one shilling and sixpence per car when two shared. The cars were numbered one to twenty-four and there was often a scramble to get a car when the ride finished.

Frank Phillips, sand artist, 'painting' Durham Cathedral on Seaburn beach *c.* 1935. Frank was a barber by trade but a serious wound to his arm in the First World War prevented him from doing his job after his return to civilian life. Frank took on any job he could manage but there wasn't much work in the 1920s and '30s. Becoming a sand artist provided an income for unemployed Frank. His son Frank jnr, recalls: 'When I was about six-years-old I would go to the beach with my dad from our house in Cooper Street, Roker. He would get down early when the tide had just gone out and claim his spot on the damp sand before anyone disturbed the smooth surface. I can remember him making out a large rectangle with his heel which provided the frame for the picture.' Frank's tools were suitable pieces of wood found on the beach and strong wire forced into the shape of a fork.

Friends and relations enjoying a day out at Roker in 1930. In the group are members of the Phillips', Philliskirk's, Douglas' and Wayman's, families. Frank Phillips, the sand artist, is in the front at the right. Behind Frank is Paul Wayman who was also a sand artist.

Frank Phillips' work is difficult to make out from the angle of this view at the Cat and Dogs Steps in the 1930s. His son Frank said that it would have been a double drawing of Durham Cathedral and York Minister, or perhaps a castle. There were four good spots for the sand artists to work: On either side of the steps opposite the Seaburn Hotel, the Cat and Dog Steps at Roker, and next to Roker Pier. The site of the drawing was always near to an elevated promenade or the pier so that people could get a good view. The drawing was difficult to appreciate at ground level. A large circle was drawn nearby and inside of it were the words 'Thank you' where passers-by threw coins.

Sand artists and family plodging at Roker, c. 1930. Centre is Frank Phillips and his brother-in-law Paul Wayman is on the left. Although Frank stopped producing his pictures on Seaburn and Roker beaches when they closed in 1939, Paul continued to please the crowds with his work after the war. From his invalid's bed in October 1980, seventy-six-year-old Paul Wayman recalled, that just after the First World War he was passing the time away on the beach by drawing a picture in the sand with a stick when passers by threw down pennies from the promenade. Paul realised that becoming a regular sand artist was a way to earn some extra money from the crowds that visited the seafront.

The County Golf Ranges Company's driving range under construction near Dykelands Road in 1965. The golf centre opened in May 1965 and also included a 18 hole putting course, a floodlit nine hole par three course, and a machine which gave golfers the effect of playing on world famous courses. However, in November 1967 the equipment was auctioned to pay off the company's debts. In April 1968 vandals attacked and torched the Seaburn golf centre causing £5,000 worth of damage.

Go Carts on Seaburn car park, 20 January 1967. A temporary track had been set up so that council officials could monitor sound levels from the nearby South Bents estate. Sunderland Planning Committee agreed to allow a permanent track to be built subject to council approval, but the company that owned the go carts began to construct the track before permission was given. The council stopped the work and finally rejected the plan in July 1967 when it was decided that there would be too much noise for local residents during race meetings.

The miniature railway at Seaburn in August 1966. The 15 inch gauge model of the London, Midland, Scottish locomotive Royal Scot was bought by the Corporation around 1955. The steam train was a popular ride and was known to Wearsiders as 'Bonnie Prince Charlie'. (See aerial view of railway track on p. 67.) In 1963 the Corporation converted Prince Charlie to diesel and it operated on the railway until 1969 when the track was removed. Bonnie Prince Charlie came into the possession of a group of enthusiasts at Haswell who ran it on their miniature North Eastern Railway.

The first train for Seaburn's new 'little railway' on its trials in August 1944. The American style steam engine was bought by Sunderland Corporation for £275. The railway was bought and laid out for a further £150, and the engine house cost £75.

In a beauty competition held at the Roker Hotel, as part of the events organised for the Sunderland Illuminations, twenty-year-old Debra Quinn was crowned 'Queen Of Lights' in September 1986. The illuminations returned to the seafront in September 1986 after a 'blackout' of thirty-two years. (See pp. 79-81.) The ten week illuminations in 1986 were considered to be something of a gamble, but which became a staggering success. The lights made the town a tourist attraction once again and about two and a half million people visited the seafront to see the lights. Sunderland was presented with a Certificate of Merit, a top tourist award, by the British Tourist Authority for the 1986 display.

The Echo Bonny Baby Contest was held in the Roker Hotel on Saturday 3 September 1988. Overall winner Lauren Wilkinson is at the front with her mother Catherine. The other winners of their age groups are, left to right: Claire Richardson and her mother Patricia, Billy Jo Duncan and mother Victoria, Melanie Elliot and mother Mary.

Six
Notarianni's

A Move to Sunderland ... The Family ... Finest Ices ... Knickerbocker Glory ... War, Internment and Separation ... Cornets and Monkey's Blood ... A Place to Meet ... 1950s Crowds ...

The Notarianni family in about 1933. Back row, left to right: Gino, Maria (maid from Italy) Egideo, Lavinia (mother), Benedetto (father), founder of Notarianni Bros (Sunderland) Ltd. Front row: Eva, Egnese, Italia. Benedetto Notarianni was the eldest of seven brothers and he emigrated to Britain in the early 1900s to work in his uncle's cafe in Glasgow. Benedetto originated from Valvori a small village in southern Italy, near Cassino. He returned to his homeland to fight for the Allies in the Great War. After the war Benedetto returned to Scotland to open a small business in Paisley. His brothers followed him in ones and twos when the business expanded. In 1923 Benedetto married Lavinia who was also from Valvori. Shortly afterwards the family moved to Sunderland and Benedetto opened a shop in Silksworth Row. Several Italian families had already settled in Sunderland when Notarianni's arrived. Pucci, Valenti, Guidi, Someo and Geraldi were established ice cream makers and salesmen. Despite being competitors they became good friends with the Notarianni family. Benedetto's brothers followed the move south and opened ice cream parlours in South Shields and Houghton. The Silksworth Row business was sold to brother Luigi, when Benedetto opened a parlour on the north side of High Street West. Benedetto moved again in 1938 when Marks and Spencers bought them out to expand their premises. Notarianni's opened an ice cream parlour and factory on the south side of High Street where they stayed until the business closed in 1988. As well as the shops which developed at the seafront Notarianni's opened the Bis-Bar in Park Lane in the early 1960s. The Bis-Bar became a popular coffee shop and restaurant that was well known on Wearside.

A postcard from the late 1930s showing seafront scenes and the exterior and interior of Notarianni's Seaburn ice cream parlour in Queen's Parade. Other families who opened for business at the new shopping complex in Queen's Parade included Atkinson, Guidi and Wright. A town council official said to Benedetto that he was courageous to open a purpose built shop at Seaburn because the area was under developed and there was nothing there. Things changed though and Seaburn took off, but Benedetto and the other families in Queen's Parade had foreseen that.

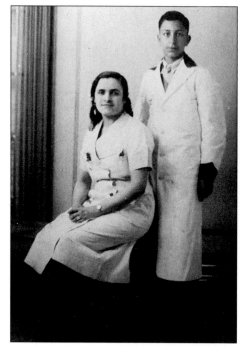

Gino and his aunt Elvira at the Seaburn premises in August 1938. Seaburn was reinforced with staff and family members from the High Street shop at peak periods during the summer months. Notarianni's also had a shop on the lower promenade at Roker, and during the 1930s illuminations they also did business from a kiosk in Roker Park.

Notarianni's first shop in Silksworth Row, August 1931. Cara Mullen, later Kingsley, (see lower photograph) is in the back row eighth from left. Luigi Notarianni sold the Silksworth Row business to Fella's and moved to Blackpool where Notarianni still trade today. Other brothers moved from Sunderland and established successful businesses at Hastings, Ramsgate and Eastbourne.

Cara Kingsley (nee Mullen), standing in the centre, began work for the Notarianni family when she left school in 1931. Cara worked for the family for fifty-seven years progressing to supervisor and manager, as well as making the ice cream. On the right is Hilda Robson who worked for the firm for forty-one years.

Benedetto Notarianni (1892-1962).
Benedetto, Lavinia and their six children took
a holiday in Valvori, Italy in the late 1930s.
Benedetto and Gino returned to Sunderland
and the rest of the family intended to follow.
The family were caught up in the war,
however, and there followed years of
separation. Lavinia and the five children were
trapped in Italy, and after Mussolini's speech
in June 1940 Italy entered the war. Benedetto
and sixteen-year-old Gino wondered what
would happen to them. There was anti Italian
feeling in the town and police dispersed a
crowd which had gathered to shout abuse and
threats outside of Notarianni's shop in High
Street West. Benedetto was detained by the
police with about twenty Italian nationals
living in Sunderland, and he was interned on
the Isle of Man.

Lavinia and five children were
separated from Benedetto and
Gino for about six years. They
were allowed to communicate by
brief messages like this one
through the Vatican, dated
September 1943. Translated it
reads: 'We are all well and we
hope to hear from you as we have
had no news from you since
September. We are in our old
house. We have asked the person
in Rome to let you have our
news.' In another message
transmitted through the Brazilian
Embassy in London dated 24 July
1940, shortly after Benedetto had
been interned, Lavinia wrote: 'I
have received news of you and
your father. Courage.'

99

A Notarianni family get together at Seaburn, Christmas, c. 1952. Back row: Gino and wife Maria, Eva and husband Charles, Cristoforo. Front row: Italia, Marisa (granddaughter), Benedetto, Lavinia holding granddaughter Lidia, Egideo, Egnese at front. Egideo was eight-years-old when war broke out, and he recalls that when he returned to Sunderland, aged fourteen, he had forgotten how to speak English. 'I had good memories of the seafront and I looked forward to coming back,' said Egideo in January 1997. 'Everything had changed in Sunderland when we returned.'

Seaburn promenade and beach, c. 1955. The Notarianni family business thrived and expanded during the post war years, particularly at Seaburn where large crowds were attracted to the developing seafront.

Notarianni's ice cream parlour and passing crowds, summer, c. 1955. If you look closely at the extreme left, two girls are crossing the road and returning to the beach. The one wearing the bathing costume is carrying a cornet having been served from the hatch window at Notarianni's.

Hot water for teapots, and chips at sixpence per bag in the mid 1950s. Mrs Hilda Robson (see the lower photograph on p. 98) started work as a supervisor in the newly constructed Notarianni's shop at Seaburn. Hilda said at her retirement in 1974: 'We opened for Whitsuntide in 1933 and the crowds waiting for ice creams the day before we were to open were so great that we started early and served them for an hour at tea-time … I haven't known a working day pass without someone asking for 'monkey's blood' on their ice cream.'

A close-up of the crowd queuing for fish and chips and hot water for tea, c. 1955. How many teapots can you spot? Notarianni's hired out teapots from here. Wearsiders returning to the beach with full pots of tea was a common sight, but the practice disappeared years ago.

A reunion of Notarianni workers took place at Humbledon and Plains Farm Workmen's Club on 15 January 1997 to celebrate the 80th birthday of Cara Kingsley. Cara recalled that the Notarianni family were lovely people to work for. 'In the late 1950s they sent Hilda Robson, Bella Sermon, Bessie Quinan and I to Italy for a holiday as a reward for twenty years service with the firm.' The town centre and Seaburn ice cream parlours were meeting places for young couples before they went to dance halls, the fair or the pictures. Many romances blossomed and marriages resulted from first meetings at Notarianni's. 'I met my husband George in the High Street shop,' said Cara.

Seven
Life Savers

Roker Volunteers … Heroism … Shipwrecks …
Breeches Buoy … The Orion … Billy Burton …
Tragedy at Roker … Lifeguards …

1. A Breeches Buoy.—2. Carrying the Apparatus.—3. Rocket and Tripod.—4. Fine Weather Costume.—5. Stormy Weather Costume.—6. Practice on the Pier in presence of the Earl of Durham.

THE SUNDERLAND VOLUNTEER LIFE BRIGADE | the North Pier, about seventy members responding to the roll.

An Illustration from *The Graphic*, an illustrated London newspaper, 6 April 1878, of Sunderland Volunteer Life Brigade. In the days of sailing ships and poor navigational aids numerous vessels were blown ashore during storms. The rocks at Roker and Whitburn Steel were particularly treacherous where floundered ships were battered. Lifeboats couldn't approach the stricken vessels and men lost their lives in full view of people standing helpless on the shore. The appalling loss of life must have had a profound effect upon locals for when the call came for volunteers to form a life brigade in Sunderland, so many men came forward that five companies were formed in 1877. Three companies operated on the south side of the harbour and two on the north side. All went under the name of Sunderland Volunteer Life Brigade and led by Captain Coulson. It was through his enthusiasm that the Brigade came into being. In 1878 the working members numbered 140, but what kind of a man joined the Brigade? In the first winter there were no watch houses and brigadesmen kept watch on the sea from the pier in open bitter conditions (see above illustration No. 5) They risked their lives to save others when a ship came ashore. All of this was voluntary for no payments. Such was the interest in the brigade that an estimated 10,000 spectators witnessed the practice pictured above.

Opposite, bottom: Sunderland Volunteer Life Brigade at Roker. The photograph was taken before the new watch house was built in 1905. On the right are members of the Coastguard in Navy like uniforms. The men at the rear are on the carriage which contained the rocket and breeches buoy equipment. Behind the group is the Rocket House which housed the equipment. The new watch house was erected next to the Rocket House.

Roker Volunteer Life Brigade Watch House, c. 1885. Early in 1878 the River Wear Commissioners gave the north division the use of a small cabin to escape the elements and for a place to meet. But in 1880 a larger purpose built watch house was erected. The cost was raised by public subscription. However, the River Wear Commissioners required the land of the new watch house but agreed to build a much larger building for the north division at the shore end of the North Pier in 1885 (pictured above). Donations were made to fit out the house and the Roker Volunteer Life Brigade held their watches from the bay window for twenty years. The R.V.L.B. moved again in the autumn of 1905 to a better situated watch house above the Blockyard, which had been planned and built by many of the members. Comfortable accommodation was included for shipwrecked crews to sleep and eat. The move was the Brigade's final one. On 19 March 1997 the Sunderland Volunteer Life Brigade celebrated their 120th anniversary in the watch house at Roker.

Orion on the beach between the piers in 1913. The German built and owned ship was leaving the port in January 1913 in rough seas and a strong wind. A wave hit her and she headed towards the South Pier as control was lost. *Orion* struck the bottom and began to sink. The sea forced her to strike the North Pier where she split in two. The lifeboat successfully rescued the crew with great difficulty while the Roker Brigade stood by. *Orion* was towed to the position shown in the photograph where she was cut up. Her keel, however, was left in the sand and there it remained until it was removed a few years ago.

Roker V.L.B. were in action on 21 November 1927 when the steamer *Efos* tried to enter the port in a gale and in heavy seas. She was forced ashore near the North Pier at about 4 a.m. and the huge seas made it impossible for the lifeboat to get in close. The Roker Brigade fired three unsuccessful rockets to the vessel, but the fourth brought the breeches buoy into action. Seventeen seamen were rescued on that day.

Roker Volunteer Life Brigade in the early 1930s, winners of the Wearside Shield. The trophy was competed for annually by brigades on the North East Coast. The life saving equipment behind the group had been supplied by the Board of Trade. Regular monthly drills and training sessions maintained a high level of efficiency.

Brigadesman Billy Burton is presented with the British Empire Medal by the Mayor of Sunderland, Alderman Eden Johnson on 11 December 1947. The award was for Billy's part in the rescue of forty-nine men from SS *Cainglen*, which went ashore at Marsden in a gale and during the blackout on 21 October 1940. Billy Burton volunteered to board the vessel, which had split in two, to tend to a sick seaman. Billy entered the basket and hauled himself up a rope - hand over hand to the *Cainglen's* deck. The Brigade attended the *Cainglen* for twenty-two hours.

H.M.S. *Ashanti* and H.M.S. *Fame* grounded on rocks at Whitburn in October 1940. Several days before the rescue of the *Cainglen* the Brigade had been in action on 17 October 1940, but the call out was no ordinary shipwreck. Despite the secrecy at that time *The Sunderland Echo* gave a graphic account of the incident towards the end of the war: '… At 5 a.m. the Brigade was summoned to Whitburn. Their gear was loaded on to a lorry, and it was the alarm signal on one of the vessels which enabled them to locate her. Over ploughed fields to the cliff they went and got themselves and the gear entangled in barbed wire. The gear had to be carried a quarter of a mile which was no light task for three officers (Captains N. Wharton, F. Albion and B. Robinson), and twelve men. The ships proved to be the destroyers *Ashanti* and *Fame*, one of which was on fire. Finding they could not fire a rocket on account of oil fuel, they took the gear down to the beach - assisted now by troops, risking whether mines were there or not. By going over the rocks and getting covered with oil fuel they managed to get near enough for a line to be floated from the ship, and Captain B. Robinson and Brigadesman W. Burton waded out and secured it. The Roker Brigade had a dual task. They had to put firefighters aboard to assist in fighting the fire which was got under control. At 3 p.m. gear was removed because of an attempt to re-float the vessels on the rising tide, but this failed, and at 9 p.m. connection was again established as the weather was getting worse. All this time the military had Bren guns fixed to give the Brigade and the small vessels protection against air attack. Leaving men in watches the Brigade laid down to snatch rest in a hut, lying down in their oil smothered oilskins, but at 2 a.m. (21 hours after the Brigade had arrived) the order for 'abandon ship' was given as the sea was getting worse, and one of the destroyers was keeling over. From the two vessels the Roker Brigade brought ashore 186 men, and the South Shields Brigade brought ashore 86 - a total of 272 in all. For 32 hours the Roker Brigade was in attendance, wet to the skin and oiled up to the eyes, cold but cheerfully carrying on.' During the war the Brigade house was taken over by the Armed Forces, but on 16 December 1944 the R.V.L.B. held a supper and smoker to celebrate the handing back of the watchhouse. The regular watches and drills could take place again. Another notable date in the history of the Brigade is 31 December 1957. On this day the Sunderland South Pier Brigade and the Roker Brigade merged into one unit. The organisation returned to its single brigade status after there had been a split of several years. However, owing to new technology the demand for this specialised ship to shore rescue service has ceased in recent years.

Sunderland Volunteer Life Brigade pose in their Watchhouse in March 1977 for the Brigade's centenary. The V.L.B. has saved over seven hundred lives since its formation. The last breeches buoy rescue was on 21 January 1963 when the *Adelfotis* went aground in Tyne Harbour, and twenty-three Greek seamen were rescued. Norman Clark, pictured front row third from left, recalls that rescue: 'The *Adelfotis* was my first rescue. It was freezing and the gale and heavy seas were forcing the ship to heave from side to side. When I returned home after being on duty sand was pitted into my face so much that my wife said I looked like a stone man.'

Members of Durham County Police life saving team create an interest on Seaburn beach in August 1960. The team are about to demonstrate a rescue by reel and line followed by artificial respiration.

Robert Wood who risked his life in September 1945 to rescue seven-year-old Eric Jepson of Eden Street, Sunderland. Despite being a non-swimmer Mr Wood dived from Roker Pier into twenty feet of water to save the boy. Robert Wood was a demobbed airman from Cecil Street. When the beaches were opened again near the end of the Second World War there was a harvest of willicks to be had on Whitburn Steel, but a new generation were unfamiliar with the dangers of sudden changes in weather and a creeping tide. In April 1945 several children were rescued after being marooned by the incoming tide. Unfortunately one twelve-year-old boy was drowned on the rocks at Whitburn. In another incident in September 1949, Norman Wilson of Chester Road saved the life of eleven-year-old John Robert Bainbridge of Back Thornton Place. Conditions deteriorated rapidly when rough seas carried the boy away in a sudden mist and Norman Wilson swam forty yards to rescue him.

Lifeguard Roger Young on duty in August 1965. When the beaches were permanently opened again in 1945 the council advertised in the Employment Exchange for a lifeguard but there were no applicants. Fearing that drownings that had occurred at Tynemouth and South Shields may happen at Seaburn and Roker, the Seaburn Traders' Mutual Association arranged a meeting in July 1945 to help form the Sunderland Beach Patrol. A rota was set up of volunteers who kept watch and patrolled the beaches during the school holidays. Their objective '… was to give assistance to anyone who found themselves in difficulties while bathing.' However, there had been a voluntary organisation patrolling Sunderland beaches before the war. In the summer of 1933 Sunderland Lifeguard Corps was formed. Volunteers had to possess the Bronze Medal of the Royal Life Saving Society. By July 1933 the Corps consisted of twenty-two members.

Shocked mothers cling to their children as a drama unfolds at Roker on 12 August 1965. Thousands of holiday makers witnessed rescue attempts when a sudden change in the weather caused rough seas which swept six youths out to sea. Two boys aged thirteen and fourteen had

got into difficulties and Ann Hancill (14) swam to help them. The girl too, was soon in trouble and Norma Tindall tried to help. Ann and the two boys reached the beach but Norma was swept out to sea. Four youths called Prest, Botton, Winter and Younger bravely joined in the rescue attempt and they were followed by some men, who also got into difficulties. Alan Younger passed a lifebelt to Norma, and the heavy seas and current carried five lads and the girl half a mile out to sea. All six were clinging to two lifebelts. Meanwhile, lifeguard Jack Ramsay, aged forty-five, was drowned as he made an heroic attempt to reach the young people. Jack Ramsay of Hylton Castle Estate had been a lifeguard for seventeen years. He left a widow and three children. RAF helicopter from Acklington and a local pilot cutter eventually rescued a total of nine people from the sea.

An exhausted swimmer is helped up the steps at Roker by police after one of several rescue attempts on 12 August 1965.

Lifeguard Eric Baillie on duty at Roker the day after Jack Ramsay lost his life and twelve swimmers almost lost theirs on 12 August 1965. After the tragedy there were criticisms aimed at the organisation and lack of rescue facilities to deal with an emergency at the seafront. There had been delay in rescue services arriving; Sunderland lifeboat crew couldn't be contacted; the lifeguard boat which patrolled offshore had been discontinued; and the warning flag had not been flying at the Cat and Dog Steps. A new system introduced for the summer of 1966 included: a lookout hut was built beside the Coastguard Station on the cliff top; experienced staff were equipped with powerful binoculars; a new high speed inshore rescue boat was bought. In August 1966 a helicopter from RAF Acklington and the new rescue boat took part in a joint life saving exercise off Roker and Seaburn. Despite the improvements holiday makers at Roker were forced to make two rescues involving five people on 7 August 1969. The inshore rescue boat had been launched on both occasions but each time it arrived after the rescue was over. Another review of the rescue system was carried out by the Corporation.

Eight
Family Album
and Memories

*Donkey Rides … Candy Floss … Toffee Apples …
Bathing Belles … Happy Days … Sandy Sandwiches …
Hot Rice … Olive Oil and Vinegar …*

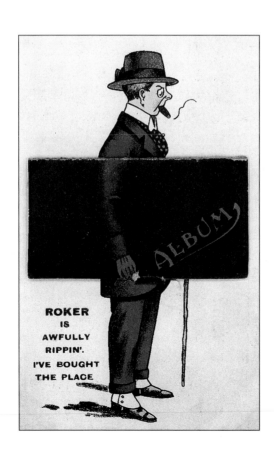

The Cockburn and Gardner families of Ferryhill on Roker beach in 1913, with two donkey boys on the right. The Holey Rock is in the background. Mrs Joan Bainbridge (nee Cockburn) of Newton Aycliffe, County Durham said: 'The photograph was taken five years before I was born. The photographer was Mr Armand Gardner who had a photography business in Church Lane, Ferryhill, County Durham. Our family often went to Roker for holidays and we stayed with relations in Sunderland.'

Susan Riddell (later Moss), aged five, and her brother Alan, aged two, of Mount Road, High Barnes playing on Roker beach in 1971. Susan was a bright girl who attended Barnes and Bede schools. She graduated with a law degree from Preston Polytechnic in 1987 and gained employment with Taylor Woodrow as a legal advisor. Susan continued her studies and became a barrister. She was 'called to the bar' in November 1989. A promotion to senior legal advisor followed and Susan worked for Taylor Woodrow on the Channel Tunnel project. A bright future was tragically cut short when Susan died of a brain tumour in November 1996, aged thirty.

Claremont House, Roker, c. 1920. Eighty-year-old Dorothie E. Stalton (nee Dugdale) remembers: 'Claremont House was formerly called Peareth House (or Grove) and it was the home of my grandfather Henry Hay Wake the engineer who designed Roker Pier. A housing estate called Peareth Grove occupies the site today. Claremont House became a private girls' school in about 1930. It stood next to Roker Lodge, a private boys' school. I attended the girls' school and one of my classrooms had been my mother's bedroom when she lived there. I was born in 1917 and my memories of my childhood at Seaburn and Roker are from the 1920s. I lived near the sea and my brother and I went down to the beach every day during the holidays. We went fishing with big nets which had long thick poles and a triangle shaped net at the bottom with a wooden blade across the front of the net which we pushed just under the surface of the sand where the shrimps hid. We would get up very early when the tide was right and shrimp all of the sandy pools and along the edge of the sea. Sometimes when the tide was really low we went along the base of the pier, and with a thick wire hook we could catch the large crabs that had hidden themselves in the rocks and crevices there. At other times, when the tide was on the turn, we fished with hand lines from the pier. You could walk right along the pier in those days. So many of the things we enjoyed as children have gone now, I'm afraid. Every day seemed to be sunny when I was a child in the 1920s. I remember the sand artist who drew marvellous pictures in the sand using a fork made of twisted wires. We would watch as Durham Cathedral appeared as if by magic. He had no photograph to help him, but there it would be with all its windows and towers as real as life. When he had finished we all clapped and threw him pennies (see pp. 90 & 91). All sorts of interesting people came down to the beach. There was the Punch and Judy man and an old ventriloquist with his doll 'Tommy'. He sat on top of a very high pair of steps, and we always expected them both to fall off as they swayed on the soft ground. We were quite sure that the doll on his knee was really talking. Sometimes a little man, would come striding along the beach playing his old tin whistle and we would join all the other children marching behind him. It really was great fun.'

Dorothie Dugdale is third from the left. Her brother Gordon is on her left. Dorothie's governess is extreme left and the Dugdale family maid, 'Little Florrie' is extreme right. Dorothie recalls: 'The Concert Party was a favourite. It consisted of people who gave shows in a large marquee on some waste land at Seaburn. Seaburn Hotel is built on it now. The same concert party came here every year and everybody looked forward to the day they arrived. It was grand. My brother and I went as often as we could. It only cost an old penny each, but that was quite a lot in those days. All of us knew everyone of the cast by name, and they knew every child too. Our greatest thrill was when someone called 'Hello' to us by name from the stage. But the one we loved best of all was the comic - 'Uncle Johnny'. Though, he too, like the rest of the troupe was expected to dance, sing, and act in all of the sketches, and of course, be a scene shifter as well. We loved to join in the singing especially the comic songs. On Sundays all the children went down to the beach at Roker where a platform had been built on the sands. There we would all join in the 'Sunshine Service'. It was a kind of Sunday School with lots of singing and grand stories. The highlight of the holidays was the carnival and fair. The roads were always crowded with people who waited for a long time for the parade to pass and you could feel the excitement of children further up the road as they heard the sound of the brass band in the distance coming nearer. Then the lorries would come and the jazz bands, not just one or two, but bands from all the pit villages around here. There were many individuals who joined in just for the fun of it, dressed up in all manner of things; clowns, tramps, men dressed as women pushing old prams containing their pals dressed as babies. You just can't imagine what bright ideas they thought up to look really funny. Others held sheets for us to throw money into for local hospitals. That wasn't the end of the day though. In the evening dad and mum took us to the fair in the Blockyard. The fair came for Carnival Week every year, and we saved our pocket money for weeks so that we could spend it there. There were roundabouts which were driven by steam engines. They played music too. There were swings and dodgem cars, and roll-a-penny. But we liked the side shows best. They were housed in small tent-like huts round the side of the field. There was the 'Fat Lady' and the 'Human Skeleton'. The 'Tattooed Man' could make the ship tattoo on his stomach look as if it was sailing by rolling his stomach muscles. There was also the 'Bearded Lady', the 'India Rubber Man', and the 'Fire Eater'. There were sideshows of working models of mines, shipyards, factories and farms. All things of wonder in those days. A small zoo came too. The only sideshow dad wouldn't let us go into was the boxing booth.'

116

Margaret Clow (later Robertson), aged six, with her sister Pauline on Seaburn beach in 1955. 'I can remember Notarianni's ice cream - the queues for a cornet with monkey's blood on it. Nothing could quite match it. A special treat was to go inside and sit there with my mam who ordered ice cream in a glass boat shaped dish. I felt so good and grand sitting beside the window, swinging my legs under the chair and watching people go by. Then we went on to the beach where I tried to work out how to put up a deck chair. I can also remember eating sandy sandwiches of egg and tomato. I loved the donkey rides but the saddle didn't seem too safe as I hung on for grim life. The day was over too quickly and I joined the long queue at the bus stop with many other tired but happy children. There was sand all over me and my damp sandy feet made my shoes hurt.'

'My mother (Gladys Shearstone) told me stories about when she was a young woman in the late 1920s, and early '30s. She is pictured on the right with her sisters on Roker beach in about 1930. My mother would get up at about 5.30 a.m. with her brothers and sisters at their home at Fulwell and go for a swim in the sea at Roker before going to work. They would swim in summer or winter regardless of the weather. They changed in the caves before the sea wall was built. One cave for girls and another for boys. My teenage years were influenced by the seafront as well. I visited the fair regularly with a group of girlfriends where we met lads, and flirted, giggled and talked. Seaburn Hall held regular 'Cats Night Out'. What a laugh that was! One night when I was about sixteen in 1966 I won a 'Cool Cats' competition. I cannot believe that I actually got up and paraded across the stage in front of all those people.'

Happy days at Roker, *c.* 1970.

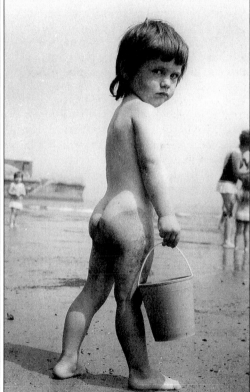

Left: 'Bathing belles' on Roker beach earlier this century. Right: A little lad at Roker, July 1971.

SANDS, SEABURN, SUNDERLAND   218467

The sands at Seaburn, *c.* 1935. Under the title of 'Exiles Return for Bank Holiday' Margaret Lennon writes: 'Along with many, many others in the 1920s a young man from Sunderland went South to look for work. He was engaged to a girl from St Mark's Road area. They married two years later and a ritual began. Summer holiday, one week only in those days, had to be spent visiting parental homes in Sunderland and also the homes of brothers and sisters. 'Wakes Week' in Otley, Yorkshire was the first week in August. That meant Bank Holiday on the beach at Roker or Seaburn. As a toddler in the early 1930s I can remember arriving at my maternal grandparents home on Bank Holiday Saturday when preparations were commencing for the big day at the beach. The men folk visited allotments for the salads and vegetables for Sunday dinner. Meanwhile, aunts and cousins arrived with their contributions of ingredients for the big baking session. Sunday dinner was a great family affair. Afterwards the women folk started baking everything from bread stotties, large cakes, small buns, to pies and tarts. My father, uncles and grandfather took all the youngsters out of the way to Barnes Park. In those days to walk sedately along through the gardens - no walking on the grass! Early Monday morning the men set out for the tram to Seaburn. They had to get the chosen site for the get together, queue for tents and chairs and erect everything for their respective families arriving with the food, buckets and spades, homemade cricket bats and balls of all sizes. My paternal grandmother with the rest of my father's siblings and their spouses arrived from Southwick and Fulwell with their additions to the meals. The games began between cousins and uncles. The ladies sitting quietly beneath big hats and long sleeved dresses ensuring no sunburn. As lunchtime approached away went some of the men to buy the jugs of tea and hot water from the kiosk on the promenade. Lunch was a hilarious affair, sand everywhere, grandparents trying to look cross, parents attempting to keep us all in order until we were told to go and play again. During the afternoon ice cream appeared from 'Notri Annie's' and eventually after more paddles, sand castles and games - tea - a repeat performance of lunch. As the sea breezes began to cool the big clear up took place and then the queue for the tram home, and every youngster washed and put to bed.'

Roker Park bandstand, 1977. Ernie Hardy recalls: 'My memories of Roker and Seaburn are mostly before 1939. My father took me to see the 'lights' in Roker Park. I was about ten years old and remember listening to Maurice Winnick and his orchestra, and Billy Merrin and his Commanders playing on the bandstand. I was fascinated being so close to these well known and popular dance bands. So much so that to this day I am a dance band fanatic, particularly with all of the bands that entertained us on the wireless of that period.'

Left: Ann and Joyce Henderson making sandcastles, *c.* 1952. Their cousin Anne Wilson, on holiday from Hertfordshire, carries buckets of sea water for a moat. Right: The three girls in a rock pool. Ethel Wilson from Yately, Hampshire recalls: 'The snaps of my daughter and her cousins bring back happy memories of the enjoyment they had over forty years ago, as my sisters and I had seventy years ago.'

120

Seaburn promenade in the mid 1950s. Jas Mutch remembers: 'My earliest memories of Seaburn was when I was very young just after the Second World War and mostly in the summer months. In those days all of the beaches were absolutely packed and we had to get there early to get a good spot. All of the family would go, and on the beach we met up with three or four other families from our area and we all had a good day out. Most families walked there and back from Southwick in those days, but it didn't seem to bother the older ones as there was a lot of fruit trees in Fulwell as we passed through, and a good bit of scrumping was done. We spent all of the day on the beach if the weather stayed fine. You couldn't afford to go on the fun fair unless an older brother or sister was working and they treated you. As I got older I would go with my older brothers picking whelks from the rocks at Whitburn. And after cooking them at home we would sell them for three old pennies a bag. Then we stopped going with our families and went to the beach with our mates instead. We would go down to the beach most nights after school, either swimming or playing football and in the summer holidays you would find us at Roker between the piers or in the North Dock. When the summer ended you would find us there again when the illuminations started. In those days we had to pay to get into Roker Park, but we used to climb over a part of the fence that wasn't guarded. Another trick was to ask courting couples for a couple of pennies saying that we had lost our bus fare, and ending up with quite a bit to spend. When I left school, and started work and had money to spend, we would go to the pub first before spending the last hour or so on the fair. We would buy cockles or mussels from the kiosks near to the fair and then take a slow walk home.'

The Heavisides family at the Cannonball Rocks in the early 1960s. Stanley Heavisides recalls: 'Our trips to the beach were always to Roker. When I was older and at school (Bede 1931-38) a lot of time was spent on the front at Seaburn. I remember one afternoon when the boys of the sixth form played Bede girls at hockey on the beach at low tide on the great stretch of sand between the Cat and Dog Steps and the Holey Rock. Of course we won but we didn't quite play to the rules. After the war, when my own children were young, we nearly always went to the Cat and Dog Steps by the Cannonball Rocks. Lots of time was spent at low tide in all the rock pools. We played cricket on the beach - what fun we had. Another game was 'Hot Rice'. All you needed was a bat and ball, or a spade, tennis racket or a piece of wood would do. Any number could play. The object of the game was to hit the batsman's body while he defended himself with the bat. If you hit him it was your turn to have a go.'

Stanley Heavisides and son Neil on Roker beach in 1952.

Sunbathing on the Cat and Dog Steps in July 1969. Looking at the camera is fifteen-year-old Barbara Allen. Barbara remembers: 'All of my spare time was spent sunbathing on the Cat and Dog Steps. It was a sun trap and we used to get there for about 7.45 a.m. for the best spot where we would get the sun all day. Further down the promenade the sun was shaded by the cliffs in the afternoon. Those who had to move back to be in the sun again found there was very little space on the crowded prom. We had a radio playing '60s music (seen in photograph) and the only time we moved was to go for some chips, or when some of the lads we knew came onto the promenade dripping wet after a swim. They would lie on us to get us wet, and sometimes they would pick one of us up and carry us into the water. The cold sea was a shock after the heat of the Cat and Dogs Steps. Bikinis soon dried out and we rubbed in some more sun tan lotion - a mixture of olive oil and vinegar. Home-time was about 7 p.m., when we looked like lobsters before we turned brown. I loved the sun and we had some great times on the Cat and Dog Steps.'

The Meechin family and in-laws on a day trip to Seaburn from Wheatley Hill, County Durham, in 1950.

Olive and Albert Walker and daughter Lynda of Hylton Castle Estate with toffee apples, c. 1956. Lynda Davison (nee Walker) remembers: 'The different smells at Seaburn stand out in my memory as a child. The sea and the aroma of freshly fried chips filled the air. I looked forward to going to the beach with my parents, but the journey was a very long one from Hylton Castle. We changed buses at Southwick where we joined a large queue at The Green. Several buses would pass by full and there was anticipation of sighting the next bus and hoping to get a seat.'

Mining families that lived near Wearmouth Colliery on Seaburn beach just after the Second World War. The friends are the Beadle, Shaw and Fowler families. Young Stan Fowler is holding the cricket bat and he remembers: 'The beach was the place to go at weekends and holidays during the summer, and the spot near Seaburn Camp was popular. On Bank Holiday's I would go down to get a tent and book our patch so early that often I have had a late breakfast on the beach.'

Barbara Collar with daughter Alison on a roundabout at Seaburn Fair in 1968. Barbara and Jim Collar and their two children moved to Wearside from London's East End with Jim's employer in 1966. 'We had no idea where Sunderland was,' said Barbara. 'But we were pleasantly surprised when we visited the seafront. Our first impression was that Seaburn was a nice, clean place with plenty of fresh air, and it was a healthy place to take the children.'

Telephone: Whitburn 78

METCALFE'S IDEAL CAFE

SEABURN

PARTIES CATERED FOR

Tents and Deck Chairs

Everything for the Beach

An advertisement from the late 1930s. Roy Elwen remembers: 'My earliest recollection of Sea Lane, later called Seaburn, are from the beginning of the 1930s. The family tent and deck chairs were kept in a large hut owned by Metcalfe's. They charged a fee for the season and my father and uncles carried them down in the spring and they would be left there until the autumn. Many families made use of this arrangement, and I believe Metcalfe's also hired out tents and chairs. Metcalfe's was just over the Borough Boundary in the then Boldon UDC and woe betide you if you took a Metcalfe tent or chair into the Sunderland part of the beach. Metcalfe's also sold tea and food, plus hot water for those who wished to make their own tea. There were several other similar kiosks along the foreshore. As the 1930s progressed the development of Seaburn took place and Metcalfe's moved over the road to a new building which is now Romanoff's restaurant.'

The recently constructed Boating Pool at Seaburn, *c.* 1938. In the boat on the left is Gordon Elwen and his sister Marjorie. The boat on the right contains eleven-year-old Roy Elwen and 'a cousin'. Notice, the miniature golf course hut in the background where golf clubs and golf balls were hired. Roy Elwen recalls: 'The Boating Pool was popular. The smell of the petrol oil exhaust was quite distinctive … During the school holidays we would go to the beach from home in Fulwell Road near Fulwell Crossing and meet up with aunts and cousins. We would get the tent from Metcalfe's and we were there for the day. At the weekend my father and uncles would be there as well. We would do the usual things like making sand castles, digging pools and going into the sea to paddle. A walk to the Steel to gather 'willicks' and examine the rock pools. Those who could swim did so. Part of the entertainment was provided by the well known Charlie Chuck and his penny whistle. There was also a ventriloquist who went back and forth along the beach, including Roker and the Cat and Dogs. He carried a pair of wooden steps and a leather suitcase which contained his dummy. The ventriloquist and dummy were dressed alike in nautical fashion - white trousers and navy-blue jacket, topped off with a peaked cap with white top. I remember him being around all through the 1930s. On the beach near the tram terminus, where the fountain is now, there were sand artists. At low tide one would draw cathedrals and castles with what appeared to be a wire fork. Another would build up sand models of animals, horses etc. Others would do the same at the Cat and Dogs (see pp. 90 & 91). And, of course, there were real ponies and donkeys. A big feature were the boat trips from the beach. At the beginning of the season wooden gangways on wheels would be towed round from the North Dock. There were several sets of these which were left throughout the summer. At night they were hauled up above the high water line. Each gangway consisted of several units of increasing height which were interconnected to reach out into the increasing depth of water. As the tide varied they were pushed out or pulled back to provide access to the many boats giving rides (see pp. 84 & 85). Most of the boats were rowing boats which provided a limited ride. There was one large motor powered boat called *Silver Spray* which took you out to the end of the pier and back. This trip cost a lot more than the rowing boats. Memory, being selective, does not recall many stormy days. It seems that the boats were there every day. In the very early 1930s it was common for unemployed men to camp on the beach at Whitburn. Perhaps they camped elsewhere as well. I remember being taken by my father to visit a friend who was camped on the beach at this time. I have since been told that families without the men present received better benefits. I have no confirmation of this.'

A pony ride on Seaburn beach in 1933. Roy Elwen, aged six, is on the left, with his brother Gordon, aged five, who doesn't look very happy. Roy Elwen also remembers: 'The walk along the prom was an entertainment. Groups laid out their tents in semi-circles and in their own little areas they would amuse themselves and the passers-by. Those with musical instruments, an accordion or banjo being popular, would have sing-songs. Energetic young men would stand on each others shoulders to form pyramids in circus fashion, and do other acrobatics. As long as the weather was fine these activities went on till quite late. At high tide we could see millions of sand eels swimming in shoals in calm water. Usually when the eels were around you would most likely see porpoises leaping out of the sea a few hundred yards away. We were told that they were after mackerel which were after the sand eels. Something that hasn't been seen for many years now. I have read somewhere that it was common for 250,000 people to visit the twin resorts in one day. The war put a stop to this, but after the war large numbers were still usual till the early 1950s.'

Seaburn beach, summer 1964. Left to right: Sandra (3), Gordon (1½) and Marie (4). Their mother Pat O'Brien recalls: 'In the 1960s, with little money and only the pram for transport, I would load up the hollow bottom of the high Churchill pram with tea and teapot, cups, sandwiches and towels. Then I piled three excited children on top and off we would go from our little cottage in Wear Street, Southwick to Seaburn where we met family and friends. If it was shipyard fortnight, and the beach was packed, I used to tie a balloon to the pram handle so family could find us easily. After an enjoyable day it was a long walk home but this time in silence with the children content and asleep in the pram.'

Novelty postcard from the 1920s. The bag opened to show twelve scenes of the seafront and Sunderland. To: Mr and Mrs Leadbetter, 11 Hearth Road, St Jude's, Plymouth. 'Dear Mr and Mrs Leadbetter. Just a PC to let you know our holiday has come to an end after three weeks at Sunderland. Had a good time, arriving back tomorrow, Tuesday. Hoping all are well.' From Mr and Mrs Avery.

A novelty postcard posted in 1965. A raised flap revealed five scenes of Roker and Seaburn and one of Mowbray Park. In the 1930s a new railway station was needed at Fulwell for the convenience of the residents of Fulwell, Southwick and Roker, and to attract more visitors to the seaside during the summer months and the illuminations during the autumn. A site was chosen to the north of Fulwell Railway Bridge and the Sunderland Seaside Development and Entertainment Committee decided to call the small station Seaburn. The new station was decorated with flags and bunting for the opening ceremony on 3 May 1937, although the occasion was overshadowed by Sunderland Football Club players who arrived at Monkwearmouth Railway Station with the FA Cup on the same day.